Making Your Point

Making Your Point

*Communicating Effectively with
Audiences of One to One Million*

David Bartlett

St. Martin's Press New York

www.stmartins.com

Library of Congress Cataloging-in-Publication Data

Bartlett, David, 1946–
      Making your point : communicating effectively with audiences of one to one million /
David Bartlett.—1st ed.
            p.   cm.
      Includes bibliographical references and index.
      ISBN-13: 978-0-312-37896-7 (alk. paper)
      ISBN-10: 0-312-37896-3 (alk. paper)
   1. Communication.   I. Title.
      P90.B324   2008
      302.2—dc22

                                                            2008009447

First Edition: June 2008

10   9   8   7   6   5   4   3   2   1

To Joan, for a lifetime of love and inspiration

Contents

Acknowledgments

I would like to thank Camille Cline for her help refining the proposal that made this book possible in the first place; my agent, Lynne Rabinoff, for making it happen in record time; and Phil Revzin for proving once again that great editors never leave fingerprints. I am also grateful for the trust and support of the many clients who have given me the opportunity over the years to practice what I preach, I hope with worthwhile results. I owe a very special debt of gratitude to all my colleagues past and present who have been so generous in sharing their insights and expertise. Above all, I am grateful to Ford Rowan and Rich Blewitt from whose accumulated wisdom and decades of experience I have borrowed liberally throughout and whose deep understanding and appreciation of the communications process inform every page of this book.

Making Your Point

Introduction

Communication is defined by the dictionary as: the "transmission of information from one person to another." Simple enough, but to paraphrase the chain gang captain's famous line in the film *Cool Hand Luke,* we have all faced situations where "what we have here is a failure to communicate." It doesn't have to be this way.

Whether you are a CEO or an intern in the mailroom, a national politician, or a college student, communication is critical. We all communicate constantly, talking on the phone, writing memos, meeting with friends and colleagues, making presentations, sometimes even giving speeches or being interviewed by the media. Most of the time we are just gathering and giving information, asking and answering questions. Often we are seeking to persuade another person to our point of view or trying get them to take a particular action. Sometimes we manage to make our points effectively. Sometimes things don't go as well as we would like.

Why is it that so many intelligent and articulate people sometimes find it so difficult to make a simple presentation to a group of clients or colleagues? Why is it that so many people who know their fields backwards and forwards sometimes find it so hard to handle a simple media interview? Why are so many people so terrified of giving a speeech? It is easy enough to appreciate why effective communication is so important to our personal and professional lives, but most of us seldom take the time to examine carefully just how we communicate and how we might do it better. We don't look carefully enough at why some communication approaches work and why others fail. We often neglect simple communications tools and techniques that are readily available and easy to use. Above all, we often fail to appreciate the single most important aspect of all successful communication, whether it be across the breakfast table or in front of an audience of thousands. We forget that effective communication is always a two-way street and that the people with whom we are trying to communicate probably have expectations very different from our own and come to the situation with an entirely different perspective.

Ordering a rebellious teenager to see things your way may be a tempting approach to a common personal communication problem, but as any parent knows, it rarely works. Carefully explaining the facts of a difficult or dangerous business situation may seem like a logical approach to a common communication problem, but, as even the most sincere and articulate executives learn the hard way every day, effective communication requires more than facts alone. Assuming that someone else will pay attention to what you say and do what you ask, just because you are who you are may seem perfectly reasonable to you, but, as you may have already discovered, this assumption often leads to nothing but confusion and disappointment. Having solid answers to all the questions you think you will be asked at a meeting or during an interview may seem like a perfectly sensible and efficient way to prepare, but unfortunately, it isn't. Understanding and appreciating the emotional dimension of communication and approaching every communications situation strategically is the only way to prevent a frustrating "failure to communicate." This book gives you the practical tools you need to succeed in this most basic of all human activities.

Volumes have been written about communications tactics, how to give speeches, how to be interviewed by the media, how to persuade someone to buy a product or take a particular action. This book begins instead by examining the more fundamental strategic considerations on which all effective communication is based. We look first at the three most basic communications challenges you face, whether you are talking with just one other person, making a speech to an audience of hundreds, or being interviewed for a news story that may reach millions. How can you get others to pay attention? How can you get them to believe what you tell them? And how can you make sure they remember what you say? We explore the importance of "emotional intelligence" in successful communication and examine why facts alone are never enough to persuade. Then we look at the Greek philosopher Aristotle's insights into the importance of basic human emotion in the communication process and how his ancient wisdom applies to today's most difficult communications challenges. Next we explore some simple but powerful tools you can use to put these fundamental communications principles into practice every day.

Since most people are far more likely to be called upon to make a point in person than they are to be interviewed by the news media, we look first at the tools you will need to prepare and deliver powerful speeches and presentations. We examine how to manage the physical and psychological stress of public speaking, how to grab and hold the attention of an audience using eye contact and body language, and how to organize a presentation for maximum impact. We show you how to relate comfortably to even very large groups by reaching them one person at a time. We show you how to prepare and use visual aids, how to use your body language as a powerful communications tool, and how to make the most of question-and-answer sessions.

Then we take a look at today's rapidly changing media landscape, including radio, television, the Internet, blogs, podcasts, online video sharing, and social networking sites. We explain how the news media really work and how you can advance your strategic communications agenda by working with them rather than allowing them to work against you. We explain how to prepare for interviews efficiently and how to achieve your communications objectives by helping reporters reach theirs. We show you tools you can use to control an interview and make sure that the point you want to make doesn't get lost in a forest of questions and answers. We look at special situations such as radio talk show appearances and high-pressure television interviews. Finally, we show you how to handle the most difficult challenge of all, communicating in a crisis situation and talking about danger and risk.

When I became president of the Radio Television News Directors Association (RTNDA), the organization had a serious problem. It wasn't the usual concern over staffing, financial stability, or membership development that small professional associations typically face. It was instead the curious fact that the nation's leading professional organization of radio and television news executives was almost entirely invisible in the very media that its powerful members controlled. As a result of this low profile, the organization lacked the influence in Washington policy debates that one might have reasonably expected it to have and that it very badly needed if it was to serve its members and its industry effectively

Because RTNDA, as a matter of policy, refused to make financial contributions to political candidates, the association found itself in the uncomfortable position of being a lobbying organization in name only, one whose voice was routinely ignored when matters of importance to electronic journalism came before Congress and the regulatory agencies. Despite this handicap, however, it still seemed odd to me and others in the RTNDA leadership that a business of such obvious importance to politicians of both parties had so little influence in political matters of such enormous importance to its future, and indeed to the survival of free expression and a free press generally. Lacking the clout that cold cash gives the typical Washington interest group, RTNDA had to find a different way to compete for visibility and impact. We had to find a different way to communicate and make our voice heard. How we eventually met this challenge taught me a great deal about the importance of strategic thinking and more specifically about the power of strategic communication.

When I first took over as president, RTNDA was a largely reactive organization. When something happened that concerned the association and its members—and given the average politician's natural antagonism to press freedom and the First Amendment, that was a frequent occurrence—the organization would make a statement pointing with pride or viewing with alarm, only to see it ignored in the media and the political community. As we analyzed the situation, two things became clear. First, RTNDA was being way too quiet. Just because it chose to avoid political partisanship didn't mean that the organization had to remain meek and silent when powerful politicians attempted, often with great success, to regulate the electronic media in ways they would never dare attempt with the print press. We also realized that RTNDA's core messages were not only unnecessarily defensive but dangerously unfocused. We quickly figured out that a single strong message delivered in a way that was memorable and quotable could attract attention and force the other side to respond. My first lesson in strategic communication was that RTNDA needed a communications offense—not just a defense, not just more effective communications tactics, but an entirely new communications strategy.

The new game plan worked. Even though RTNDA never tried to play the traditional lobbying game by helping influential politicians raise campaign contributions in exchange for their support on key issues, the association was able to get its voice heard where it counted by focusing its communications efforts strategically, targeting audiences to whom the politicians we needed to influence would listen. Regardless of the specific issue at hand, we relentlessly hammered home a single, simple message: Any form of government regulation of radio and television content is a violation of the First Amendment, no matter how cleverly or attractively it might be disguised as a public service. The details behind these arguments are complicated and legalistic, and RTNDA was always fortunate to have brilliant lawyers who could articulate the legal complexities as well or better than anyone. But from a strategic point of view the legalistic approach was usually a waste of time. It left us on the defensive and allowed politicians and regulators anxious for the government to control the content of radio and television news to shape the debate on their terms.

If we ever hoped to regain the political advantage, our message would have to be simple and positive. It would have to be instantly memorable, easily quotable, and, above all, in tune with the attitudes and emotions of the general public, not just legal scholars. So we reduced our arguments against content regulation to very simple messages such as: "Do you want politicians like Ted Kennedy and Jesse Helms telling you what you will be allowed to see on a television news broadcast?" Easy to quote. Easy to remember. Simple to understand. Absolutely nonpartisan. And very responsive to the public's emotional distrust of all politicians.

Before long, news organizations that had never heard of RTNDA were calling us for quotes and comments whenever an issue involving content regulation came up. As long as we kept our message simple and delivered it with memorable quotes, reporters kept coming back for more. Without spending a nickel on campaign contributions, our voice was finally being heard where it counted. Instead of reacting after the fact to every new assault on press freedom from Capitol Hill or the Federal Communications Commission, RTNDA was delivering its own positive message, and the politicians and regulators were starting to get calls from reporters and constituents asking them to defend their positions. Many chose to back off and go looking for easier battles to fight. Supporters of a free press were starting to win the war.

The lessons about the power of strategic communication that this experience taught me form the basis of this book. The tools that we used are here to help you make the most of the communications opportunities that come your way every day.

1/

Issues, Messages, and Emotions

A Strategic Approach to Communication

We have all wondered from time to time why it is so difficult to get people to pay attention to what we have to say, to believe us, and to remember the most important points we make. When the Greek philosopher Aristotle took a look at this problem he concluded that effective communication is really more about human nature than cold hard facts. Human nature hasn't changed that much in the past two thousand years. Emotional intelligence, the ability to understand and appreciate where someone else is coming from, is still essential to effective communication.

How was Johnson & Johnson able to maintain its credibility during the Tylenol crisis and save a product many experts assumed was fatally damaged? It had a lot to do with how well the company understood and appreciated the emotional concerns of its customers, concerns that quite literally involved life and death. More recently, why was Firestone so dramatically *unsuccessful* dealing with a very similar situation when it faced charges that defective tires had caused a string of fatal SUV accidents. Again, it was all about human emotion. Firestone failed to appreciate that the facts alone, no matter how powerful they seemed to those who understood them, would never persuade a fearful driver. Engineering data will impress an engineer, but they mean nothing to a young mother terrified that she might be putting her children's lives at risk every time she loads them into an SUV riding on Firestone tires.

Effective communication involves much more than speaking eloquently, answering tough questions, coming up with clever quotes, and staying out of trouble when talking with inquisitive reporters. Making your point in today's unforgiving information environment demands a truly strategic approach, beginning with careful consideration of those three fundamental communications challenges: getting others to pay attention to what you have to say; getting others to believe what you tell them; and getting others to remember what you have said long enough for them to act on it. For any of this to work, of course, you must have something worthwhile to say in the first place.

From a strategic perspective, communication can never be viewed as an end in itself. It must always serve a larger purpose. The most effective communication is never reactive or defensive. It is always positive and proactive. In order to take full advantage of every communications opportunity that comes your way you must always consider your big picture strategy before choosing a tactical approach. Effective communication demands that you look at every communications situation first from the outside in. Unless you thoroughly understand and appreciate the larger strategic situation and the risks and opportunities it presents, it will be difficult, if not impossible, to make wise tactical decisions.

For example, just knowing the answers to all the questions you think you might be asked in a certain situation and then being able to offer up those answers on demand does not define communications success. Neither does the ability to defend yourself against an angry questioner or an aggressive reporter trying to get you to say something newsworthy that you will soon regret. Effective communication is all about having a solid story to tell and being able to tell it in a way that will appeal to whatever audience you need to reach. The ultimate test, of course, is whether the audience you are trying to reach remembers what you say and responds as you hope they will.

The strategic questions are familiar but all too often overlooked. What are you really trying to accomplish in this particular communications situation? With whom do you need to communicate? Why do you need to reach them? What do they expect from you? Why should they even bother listening to what you have to say? What do you want them to remember? What do you want them to do? What's in it for them? What's the point you are trying to make?

Who Cares?

Just because you firmly believe that something you are about to say is important, and just because you can demonstrate factually why it should matter to the audience you are trying to reach, does not guarantee that anyone else will even pay attention, much less believe or remember your message. Be realistic with yourself and your colleagues about who is likely to care about what you say and why. Above all, understand that your job as a communicator is to make what you believe is important somehow interesting to others.

For example, in our work as consultants to corporations across the country and around the world, my colleagues and I spend a lot of time on airplanes. It is very important to all of us and, of course, to our families, that most airplanes take off and land safely most of the time. But nobody else on the planet could possibly be expected to consider it interesting, much less newsworthy. That's just human nature. Nobody watches television or reads a newspaper to be reassured that most airplanes land safely most of the time. But when an airplane crashes somewhere, whether anyone we know is on it or not, it is likely to be headline news. In order to be interesting and newsworthy, an event must by definition be unusual, out of the ordinary, bizarre, or even sensational. Good news isn't really "news" at all. And just because you can prove that something is important doesn't automatically mean that anyone else will pay attention or care.

The way the news media routinely cover politics is a perfect example. Nobody stays up late on election night anxiously waiting to learn which vision of Social Security or Medicare policy will prevail. People stay up in order to find out who won. The news media know perfectly well that issues are important in politics, but because the audience is more interested in winners and losers, they focus most of their attention on the horse race. This isn't the result of some strange flaw in the media's world view. It isn't, as some serious-minded critics would have you believe, a symptom of profound media ignorance. It is just human nature. Most of us see the world in stories, and we want those stories to be new and interesting. If a story isn't interesting or doesn't relate to our emotional concerns, we probably won't pay attention for very long, no matter how hard someone else may try to convince us of its enormous importance to our lives. Successful communicators have mastered the art of making what is important to them also interesting and important to the people they need to reach. But it doesn't happen by accident.

Effective communication is a proactive exercise. It is about playing to win, not just playing not to lose. Effective communication is about telling your story, making your point, and scoring points with your message. It is not about defending yourself against someone else's allegations. This is why merely preparing to answer tough questions is never enough. No matter how well you do it, just answering questions is mostly a defensive exercise. Someone else is setting the agenda. Someone else is in control. Effective communication is all about having a point to make, understanding why it is important, then knowing how to make it interesting and memorable, regardless of the circumstances.

Defining the Debate

Effective communication is also about something called *issues management.* The primary objective of issues management is to define the terms of a debate before someone else has a chance to do it first. Issues management supports strategic communication by helping establish a framework for the story that is as favorable as possible to your point of view and the strategic outcome you are trying to achieve. It is all about telling your story before someone else tells it for you. This is much more than an exercise in timing or semantics. If you are able to define the terms and establish the theme that shapes the story, you can control the discussion. And if you can control the discussion, you are more likely to win the debate eventually, no matter how powerful your opponent's arguments may seem at first. But if your opponents are able to shape the semantic battlefield and lay down the ground rules ahead of you, you will have a much steeper hill to climb, no matter how eloquent your message may be. Issues management, like strategic communication, is never a defensive exercise. Issues management is about establishing home field advantage and controlling the story, not just fending off difficult questions.

For example, a serious chemical plant explosion might raise a number of potentially troublesome issues, each of which could be debated from a number of different angles. The same set of facts could easily support several very different story lines, some clearly more attractive to the plant owners than others. The blast and fire might very well spark a discussion of plant safety and the potential threat the plant might pose to the surrounding community. The explosion might raise questions about potential environmental impact. It might start a discussion of the economic importance of the products the plant produces and the jobs it brings to the local community.

If your company happens to own that burning plant, it would clearly be in your best interest to see the story of the explosion and fire framed in terms of plant *safety,* rather than plant *danger.* You certainly would prefer to focus attention on how well prepared you were to deal with the accident. You would want the news media to highlight all the things your company is doing to put out the fire and protect the community. You certainly would like the neighbors to see your plant as a positive economic force rather than a risk to public health and safety. You would prefer the overall theme of the story to be about solutions not problems. Since negativity is almost always more newsworthy than anything positive, however, others will probably be looking first for the bad news.

Shaping the theme of a story is not a matter of empty spin. The facts are the facts. No amount of clever communication can put out the fire or magically turn the clock back to a time before the plant blew up. This is rather about defining the terms, framing the debate, and setting the ground rules for what inevitably will be an ongoing discussion about the plant and the accident. More than anything else, strategic communication is about influencing the tone of the coverage and shaping the theme of the story.

Definitions Matter

Think for a moment why the enormous industry that earns billions in annual profits from treating disease is called *health care,* rather than, say, *disease management.* After all, keeping people healthy and curing them of disease are really just two sides of the same coin. But most people are more comfortable talking about health than they are talking about disease. Health is positive and hopeful. Disease is negative and depressing. A company in the health business naturally has a more positive and attractive image than one that is in the disease business. Or consider companies that process meat products. When discussing what might happen if spoiled meat accidentally found its way into the supermarket, most people in the meat business would prefer to talk about *food safety* rather than *food-borne illness.* The facts are essentially the same, but for the audience the emotional connotation is very different. Talking about illness and danger is negative and defensive. Talking about health safety is proactive and positive. Especially when trying to communicate about matters of life and death, these subtle differences matter more than you might think.

Problems and Solutions

An interesting example of how this process works involves two well-known companies, once units of the same huge international conglomerate. Food processing giant Kraft and the old-line tobacco company Philip Morris have both faced serious strategic communications and issues-management challenges over the years. But they have tackled them in very different ways, and with very different results. Philip Morris and other big tobacco companies spent many years and countless millions of dollars defending themselves against charges that their primary product, cigarettes, can kill the people who smoke them. The debate went on for decades, but unfortunately for the tobacco companies, the fundamental issue involved was shaped by their opponents at the very beginning of the controversy. Antismoking activists succeeded in framing the debate around public health and product safety. As a result, the eventual outcome was settled almost as soon as the discussion began. The companies fought back, sometimes with tough tactics that have since been found illegal, but whatever they did really didn't matter once the terms of the debate had been defined by the other side. As soon as the tobacco companies were put in the position of defending themselves against charges that their products were responsible for a deadly disease and that they were willfully ignoring the danger, the debate was effectively over. It was no longer a question of whether big tobacco would lose, but only when and, of course, how much it would eventually cost them.

Now let's take a look at how Kraft has dealt with an issue that is only just starting to attract public attention, but which has the potential to be just as devastating to the food business as antismoking activism was to big tobacco. Obesity is of increasing concern to food companies everywhere. Activist groups and the plaintiffs' bar are busy raising public awareness of the problem and pointing the finger of blame at big food companies, accusing them of ignoring public-health concerns in an effort to get us all hooked on unhealthy junk food. Kraft could have wasted a lot of time and money arguing that none of the food products it sells, by themselves, could possibly make anyone fat or unhealthy. They could have tried to convince the public that obesity is

simply caused by eating too much. But as the debate got underway in earnest, Kraft took a very different approach.* Instead of
arrogantly dismissing public-health concerns the way the tobacco
companies did for so many years, Kraft tried hard to be sensitive
to the concerns and values of those whose opinions will determine who ultimately prevails in the obesity debate. There is
plenty of evidence available to support the contention that obesity
is more about overeating and lack of exercise than it is about unhealthy food. But rather than blame their customers for the problem, or try to fight human nature, Kraft acted voluntarily to restrict
advertising to children and take other measures to promote healthy
eating habits.

Kraft could have marshaled its considerable scientific expertise
to make a powerful case that public opinion and conventional wisdom are all wrong and that the food products Kraft sells are in no
way responsible for the nation's rapidly expanding waistline. The
company could have used irrefutable factual evidence to argue that
growing popular concern about obesity is not based on sound science, or even common sense, but on irrational fear stirred up by
greedy trial lawyers looking for new industries to sue. Those arguments might be accurate, and for someone running a multi-billion-
dollar food business, very tempting to make. But they would never
be persuasive, at least not with the vast majority of ordinary people
who would much prefer to blame all those unwanted pounds on a
big corporation rather than their own bad eating habits.

In another example, one of Kraft's competitors, Kellogg, despite a long history of promoting health and wellness, found itself
on the wrong end of a $2 billion lawsuit charging that its products

---

* Sarah Ellison, "Why Kraft Decided to Ban Some Food Ads to Children," *Wall
Street Journal,* October 31, 2005.

contribute to poor nutrition in children.* Assuming its healthy reputation would be enough to deter uninformed critics, Kellogg ignored obvious warning signs that it might become the target of a well-organized special interest campaign designed to capitalize on growing public concern about nutrition. In retrospect, the company should have told its healthy food story much sooner and much more aggressively. Instead, it largely ignored the public relations risks posed by its marketing initiatives aimed at children and ended up getting sued, in part because it allowed others to capture the high ground in the larger debate over nutrition and health. When the chips are down it is always better to be perceived as part of the solution than part of the problem.

Many years of research have established quite clearly that most people worry too much about all the wrong things, even as they blithely ignore real risks to their health and safety. Just because they have their facts all wrong, however, doesn't mean that their unfounded fears are any less real, at least to them. Just because a strong scientific case can be made that many factors other than processed foods are responsible for the nation's epidemic of obesity doesn't mean that people who are sincerely concerned about public health and nutrition won't go looking for someone other than themselves to blame for the obesity problem. Big companies that make millions selling processed foods are an easy target. When someone asked the gangster Willy Sutton why he robbed banks, Sutton famously replied, "Because that's where they keep the money." These days, the plaintiffs' bar lives by very similar rules. Businesses big and small have no choice but to stay alert for emerging issues that might make them easy targets for special

---

* "How Kellogg Ignored Warning Signs of Food Lawsuit," *Advertising Age* Web site, January 25, 2006, http://adage.com/article.php?article_id=48220.

interest campaigns that, if not handled carefully, could create potentially devastating legal liability and do serious damage to their corporate reputation and bottom line. That's what issues management is all about.

Verifiable facts and powerful arguments aside, it rarely makes sense to swim against the tide of popular opinion and conventional wisdom, no matter how ill informed the general public may be. It rarely makes sense to dismiss the deeply held values of those you are trying to reach, even if you are convinced, on the strength of overwhelming factual evidence, that those values are utterly irrational and entirely misplaced. It is far better to do what Kraft did when it first spotted obesity emerging as a potentially dangerous issue: Listen very carefully to your audience; get in touch with their most deeply held values and opinions; be sensitive to what worries them and why; show respect for their emotional concerns; try to find common ground; and above all, try to frame the emerging debate on your terms and in a way that will resonate with those who will ultimately determine your fate. If you succumb to the perfectly natural temptation to defend yourself aggressively against unfair and uninformed accusations, you will just be joining the debate on your opponent's terms. The very best you can hope for is a draw, and then only if you are very lucky, or your adversary's arguments are especially weak. Framing the debate on your terms at least gives you a chance to score points, even if the other side's arguments at first appear to be extremely strong.

Intel Inside

What happened to the highly respected microchip manufacturer Intel late in 1994 is a good example of how verifiable facts and common sense are rarely enough to win a high-stakes debate with customers or the competition.* Intel's problem began to emerge quietly, so quietly that almost nobody at the company bothered to pay much attention. A mathematics professor in Virginia noticed that Intel's latest Pentium computer chip was prone to errors in what are called floating-point calculations. The ability to handle these complex arithmetic processes is built into most of today's processor chips, but only a tiny fraction of personal computer users would ever have occasion to use the function or even know about it. As it turned out, Intel engineers had already spotted the floating-point bug long before the professor did, but they chose to ignore it. Being engineers with a solid grasp of technology and statistics, they were able to estimate quite accurately that the average spreadsheet user might encounter a problem with the Pentium floating-point calculation once every 27,000 years. Hardly worth worrying about. Hardly worth worrying about, that is, until word of the newly discovered Pentium bug hit the Internet and instantly became the talk of the personal computer world. Within days, an insignificant technical problem of interest only to computer engineers and a tiny fraction of sophisticated PC users became a national news story about the shortcomings of a well-known consumer brand. At first, Intel's engineers reacted just like engineers. Oblivious to the broader implications of what they still believed to be an arcane technical issue, they weighed in with solid technical facts. They weren't trying to hide anything, at least not anything they believed to be worth worrying about. Their initial message to consumers was simple and sincerely intended to be reassuring. Relax, unless you frequently need to manipulate huge numbers on your computer, you will never even notice the floating-point problem.

---

* Richard S. Tedlow, "The Education of Andy Grove," *Fortune,* December 12, 2005, 137–38.

What the engineers failed to realize was that Intel was no longer just in the business of supplying complex components to personal computer manufacturers. Once Intel reached out to the broader consumer market by advertising "Intel Inside" as a key component of just about every Windows PC, the company's audience changed significantly. So did that audience's perceptions and expectations of Intel as a company. Intel's primary audience was no longer the computer designers and manufacturers to whom it had always sold its chips. The company's audience was now dominated by millions of ordinary consumers with very little patience for big companies that make complicated excuses for flawed products. By promoting the Intel Inside brand, Intel had moved from the wholesale microchip business into the retail PC business, where personal computers are considered just another consumer product and where the companies that make them are seen as no different than those that manufacture low-tech appliances like toasters and dishwashers.

Thanks to its long experience in the consumer market, IBM, a major purchaser of Intel Pentium chips for its line of personal computers, was a lot quicker to realize what was really going on. The verifiable technical facts notwithstanding, ordinary consumers were having a serious emotional problem buying computers with a known flaw, even if they were perfectly able to understand intellectually that the bug wouldn't show up to bite them for three hundred centuries. While Intel was still trying to explain why the floating-point problem was not really a problem at all, IBM unilaterally announced that it would not ship any more PCs with Pentium chips until the bug was fixed.

That got Intel's attention, and within days the company announced a no-questions-asked replacement policy. But old habits and beliefs often die hard. Intel's statement said:

What we view as a minor technical problem has taken on a life of its own. We apologize. We were motivated by a belief that replacement was simply unnecessary for most people. We still feel that way.

In other words, "We're the experts. We're right. We're smart. You, the people who buy our products and pay our salaries, are dumb." Intel was absolutely right on the facts. To a computer engineer those facts were never in doubt. But the technical details didn't matter one bit to ordinary people considering whether to buy personal computers containing Pentium chips, and it was those people who now held Intel's fate in their hands. As engineers, the top executives of Intel, including the company's legendary CEO, Andrew Grove, just couldn't, or perhaps wouldn't, see the world through the unsophisticated and, to them, irrational eyes of their customers. They were unable to set aside their technical expertise and attitudes long enough to appreciate their customers' emotions. They casually dismissed the values and beliefs of their customers because, in their judgment, those values and beliefs ran counter to the verifiable facts. Facts they considered too obvious to question. In the end, recalling those slightly imperfect Pentium chips cost Intel $475 million and taught the company, and anyone else who was paying attention, a harsh lesson about the importance of emotion in driving public debate.

Smoke Gets in Your Lungs

A similar situation presented itself when we represented a coalition of big diesel engine manufacturers in their battles with clean air advocates who consider diesel exhaust to be a major source of dangerous air pollution. The scientific facts are complicated, but the political situation was all too simple and obvious. The diesel industry was being deliberately portrayed as a bunch of rich, insensitive companies reaping enormous profits by pouring tons of deadly soot into the lungs of innocent children.

For their part, the diesel companies had a strong case to make, not only for the enormous importance of diesel power to the nation's economy, but also for the technological breakthroughs that were rapidly making their diesel engines every bit as clean as any other internal combustion power source. The diesel manufacturers naturally wanted the debate to be about cutting-edge technology, a new lease on life for the venerable and valuable diesel engine. Opponents of diesel power preferred to shroud the rational scientific discussion in a cloud of smelly black smoke. They wanted the debate to be about death, disease, and the need for immediate regulation of diesel exhaust. They didn't want to participate in any discussion about new technology or whether it made sense to regulate the manufacture and sale of diesel engines and diesel fuel. They wanted the debate to be only about how quickly and how vigorously those regulations could be put in place and enforced. The stakes were potentially enormous, both for the nation's heavily diesel-dependent economy and for vehicle manufacturers who were counting on a new generation of diesel engines to help them meet the government's increasingly stringent fuel economy standards.

The diesel manufacturers could easily have rolled out volumes of technical and economic data in an effort to make their case on the hard facts—and at first they did just that. But they soon recognized that complex scientific data, no matter how convincing to engineers, are simply no match for powerful visual images of big trucks belching huge clouds of black smoke into the air. Abstract economic arguments about the importance of diesel power, no matter how well founded, are no match for the sad, pale faces of little children suffering from asthma attacks.

Opponents of diesel were telling anyone who would listen, especially antibusiness politicians, that diesel smoke is a direct and significant cause of cancer, asthma, and a host of other deadly diseases. Their scientific evidence was shaky, but their story was visually powerful, emotionally compelling, and very memorable. They knew how to play to the public's fears and generate sensational news coverage. They knew they would have a much better chance of winning in the long run if they made sure the debate was about smelly black smoke and deadly disease rather than sound economics or the marvels of modern diesel technology. They understood that serious and substantive public policy debates are often won or lost with catchy sound bites, strong visual images, and emotionally compelling news coverage.

Rather than argue that the impact of diesel pollution on public health should be weighed thoughtfully against the economic benefits of diesel power, the companies chose instead to focus on promoting what they decided to call *clean diesel.* Manufacturers of modern, clean-diesel engines sought to embrace the emotional concerns of the audience and thereby frame the debate in a new and potentially more favorable light. They worked to shift the discussion away from the ravages of disease and toward the wonders of new technology. They chose to focus on shared concerns about clean air rather than bitter debates over the relative danger of fine particle pollution. They chose to talk about cutting-edge solutions rather than depressingly familiar problems.

News Coverage and Public Opinion

The story of the diesel technology debate highlights something else that anyone dealing with an intrinsically negative issue should always keep in mind. Negative news coverage, in and of itself, need not drive overall public opinion in a negative direction. Most of us do, in fact, think positively about most issues most of the time. Most of us don't want the world to fall apart and don't really expect it to do so any time soon. Those of us who don't have an immediate personal stake in the outcome of a particular debate really would like to see things work out well for everyone involved.

Nevertheless, it is hard to imagine any positive story about a possible link between air pollution and lung cancer. In this case there was nothing anyone on the prodiesel side of the debate could do to generate positive stories about disease and death. But careful tracking of public opinion trends, along with continuous in-depth analysis of the actual content of media coverage about diesel fuel, air pollution, and health effects over the same period of time, revealed that positive messages can move public opinion in a positive direction, even when those positive messages appear in otherwise entirely negative news stories.

The diesel debate is an instructive example of why it pays to promote a positive message rather than mount a defensive campaign against your opponent's position. Negative and defensive messages only push public opinion further in a negative direction. Being defensive leaves your audience with the impression that you probably have something to be defensive about. It makes people think that all those negative things your opponents are saying about you might somehow be true, no matter what rational arguments you are able to make to the contrary.

Generating positive stories about ugly diesel exhaust would have been next to impossible. Getting the positive clean-diesel message into the ongoing coverage was a lot easier, and considerably more effective. Not surprisingly, continuous media content analysis showed that the overall tone of news stories about diesel power and diseases caused by air pollution remained overwhelmingly negative from start to finish. Stories about disease and pollution are always going to be negative. But simultaneous public opinion polling showed a significantly positive reaction to messages about clean diesel, regardless of the context in which they happened to appear. At the very least, positive, proactive messages have a chance of being considered favorably by those in the target audience who are genuinely undecided, and that is usually the vast majority.

Rather than fold its tent and withdraw from the debate, or fight back from a defensive crouch, the diesel industry coalition took the high road and kept delivering its positive message about how new diesel technology was helping clean up the air that we all breathe and deal with pollution concerns we all care about. Public opinion responded positively. Positive messages about clean-diesel technology moved the public opinion meter in a positive direction, even in the face of otherwise overwhelmingly negative news coverage. Today, a majority of the general public is either neutral on the issue or sees diesel power as part of a possible solution to the nation's energy problem.

2 /

Advice from Aristotle

Communication and Human Nature

Aristotle taught that facts alone, no matter how compelling, will rarely persuade an audience, especially a fearful or skeptical audience. Indeed, the facts alone will not even get most people to pay attention. Effective communication is about getting in touch with what makes people mad, sad, or scared. Aristotle's great contribution to our understanding of communication was his recognition of the importance of human nature and human emotion. Aristotle taught that in order to reach the minds of other people and have an impact, your message must first touch their hearts and hit their guts. Two thousand years later, Benjamin Franklin came to a very similar conclusion, writing in *Poor Richard's Almanack*: "Would you persuade, speak of Interest, not Reason."* Aristotle and Franklin both understood

---

* Benjamin Franklin, *Poor Richard's Almanack 1734*, http://www.vlib.us/amdocs/texts/prichard34.html.

that effective communication is always less about you than it is about those you want to reach. What matters to you, even if it matters a lot, is far less important than what matters to them. What you say is far less important than what they hear, what they remember, and ultimately, how they feel.

Facts alone, no matter how well supported or attractively packaged, are rarely powerful enough on their own to overcome deeply felt emotions. Effective communication must therefore be firmly anchored in the emotions of the audience. It must be about more than just delivering useful information. And it must be about more than just getting people to do what you want; that's just a matter of the strong ordering around the weak. In the long run, effective communication is about reaching others on their terms rather than yours. Above all, effective communication requires a sensitive understanding and appreciation of basic human nature, something that is all too easy to overlook in the search for clever messages and creative ways to deliver them. In order to communicate effectively you must first understand and appreciate what worries your audience and why, what might motivate them to take some sort of action, and why anything you say might make a difference in their lives. If Aristotle or Franklin were around today, they would undoubtedly pose exactly the same three basic questions we all ask when deciding whether to pay attention to what someone else has to say: So what? Who cares? What's in it for me?

Many psychologists consider Aristotle the true father of their discipline because he was the first to organize observed human emotion in an orderly, scientific framework. Aristotle did this not as an abstract philosophical exercise or as a form of primitive psychotherapy, but for the very practical purpose of figuring out how to persuade people at an emotional level. When Aristotle compiled his great treatise on persuasive communication,* the stakes for communicators were very high indeed. In classical Athens even the most serious legal disputes were settled by appeal to a public gathering of all the adult male citizens of the city. An Athenian's life, liberty, and property might well depend on his ability to persuade an audience of hundreds of his fellow citizens. There were no lawyers. An Athenian pleading his case was required to speak for himself and submit his arguments to the judgment of the crowd. When Aristotle wrote his communications handbook he was not indulging in idle philosophical speculation. He was offering his students very specific advice about how to make an audience listen, believe, remember, and act.

Making Your Message Effective

Aristotle taught that the most effective messages are always positive, concrete, and empathetic. Strong messages are never defensive. If you find yourself under attack, your first reaction will probably be to defend yourself as vigorously as you possibly can. But if your message sounds defensive, a skeptical audience will probably assume you have something to be defensive about, even if you are making a strong, logical case supported by powerful evidence. Along the same line, the most effective messages are those that explain what you are doing now and what you are committed to doing in the future. They are rarely about what you did or wished you hadn't done at some point in the past, or what you solemnly promise never to do again. Just because someone else may try to frame an issue with a negative spin doesn't mean you should respond the same way. Regardless of the situation, you

---

* *Aristotle on Rhetoric: A Theory of Civic Discourse,* trans. George A. Kennedy (New York: Oxford Unversity Press, 1991).

should always try to resist the natural temptation to defend your-self against false accusations and negative insinuations. Taking a positive and proactive approach will help frame the discussion on your terms and make whatever message you eventually decide to deliver far more effective in the long run.

Effective messages are always supported by credible evidence. Abstract concepts are just too hard for most people to process. It is always easier to relate to something specific and concrete. Going back to that exploding chemical plant, the most important audiences, at least in the short run, are looking for a lot more than abstract assurances that the company knows what it's doing and they have nothing to fear. These people are afraid for their lives, and they want to know exactly what you are doing to deal with the problem. They want to feel that you will keep them safe. They want to be assured that they are not going to die. For example, a typical generic standby statement about how the company is "do-ing everything possible to protect the community" would be much stronger if it included specifics, such as "we already have 150 firefighters on the front line, and they have contained the blaze to section A20 of the property, nearly a mile from the near-est neighbor."

Above all, Aristotle taught that effective messages are always empathetic. They always reflect a sensitive understanding and sin-cere concern for what matters most to the target audience. Effec-tive messages are never about you and your agenda. They are always about the concerns of those you are trying to reach. You and your organization have priorities and concerns, of course, but like the rest of us, the people you need to reach care first and fore-most about themselves. That's just human nature. Understanding and appreciating the concerns of your audience will make a signif-icant difference in how effective your messages will be at making your point, persuading the audience to your point of view, and helping you reach your strategic objective.

Caring, Commitment, and Action

The most effective messages, especially when the circumstances are difficult and the stakes are high, always include statements to the effect that "we care, we are committed, and we are taking action." When the pressure is on, assuring someone else that you care about what worries them is much more than common courtesy. Sincerely identifying yourself with the concerns of your audience is crucial to the ultimate effectiveness of your message. In order to hold the audience's attention and preserve your credibility, you must show that you sincerely respect their values and share their concerns, even if the facts as you understand them suggest that those concerns are completely unfounded.

For example, the safety record of nuclear power plants in this country is easily verifiable. There have been accidents, of course, but not very many and none that has ever resulted in a fatality or any significant harm to anyone living near a nuclear plant. But just try convincing someone who actually lives near one of those plants that they are perfectly safe. Statistics notwithstanding, people who live near the plant know perfectly well that if something ever did go wrong it would be their children who would be glowing in the dark, not yours. It would be their lives on the line, not yours. Against that emotional background, how could you possibly expect anyone to believe anything you say about nuclear plant safety on faith alone, no matter how well the facts may support you? Anything you say will almost certainly be greeted with skepticism or worse, unless you are very careful always to show sincere respect for the concerns of the audience. Remember the story about the hog, the chicken, and a bacon-and-egg breakfast. When it comes to bacon and eggs, the chicken is interested. The hog is involved. Those with an emotional involvement in an issue and a personal stake in the outcome are more than just interested. Like the hog, they are involved.

Tragedy at Crandall Canyon

The mine collapse that claimed the lives of six coal miners and three rescue workers in Utah in the summer of 2007 is an excellent example of how good intentions alone cannot guarantee effective communication in an emotionally charged situation. When six miners were trapped by a collapse in the Crandall Canyon coal mine, co-owner Robert Murray was quick to appear on the scene in person. Murray immediately took charge of the rescue operation and all communication with families, the community, and the media.

Murray was an outspoken and often controversial figure, eager to defend the mining industry and well known for run-ins with environmentalists, labor unions, and government officials. His decision to take command of the situation at the mine was met with a mixed reaction. On the one hand Murray was criticized for elbowing government experts out of the way. At the same time, however, many people praised him, at least initially, for standing up and taking responsibility for the situation himself rather than trying to hide behind underlings or outside consultants. For reporters looking for fresh angles to an increasingly grim story, Murray's personal history was also interesting. He had been a miner himself and had once been trapped in a mine collapse. When he recounted that experience to reporters and told them how frightened he had been it added significantly to his credibility. But then the rescue effort began to stall. No signs of life were found in the area where the miners were thought to be trapped. A second cave-in killed three rescue workers and injured several others. And critics began to make their voices heard about Murray's past history as an apologist for the mining industry and an owner and operator of nonunion mines with a record of safety violations.

Murray's initially positive image as a man willing to take responsibility and deal forthrightly with a difficult situation shifted quickly to that of a greedy and heartless employer willing to cut corners and put other people's lives at risk to line his own pockets. Meanwhile, faced with the increasing pressure of a rapidly deteriorating situation, Murray let his outspoken and abrasive personality get the better of him, bashing the media, accusing union organizers of mischaracterizing his company's safety record, and condemning critics of coal mining as disloyal to the American economy. The facts of the situation at Crandall Canyon hadn't changed substantially, but a lot of what Murray had said previously came back to haunt him.

In the early hours of the rescue Murray stated emphatically that the mine collapse had been caused by a small earthquake, something over which he and his company obviously had no control. When seismologists questioned whether the seismic activity their sensors had detected around the time of the disaster was the cause of the mine collapse or merely the result of it, Murray angrily dismissed their interpretation. Reporters, government officials, and most importantly, the families of the trapped miners, began to wonder whom to believe, a mine owner or the scientific experts. As things grew steadily more desperate at the mine, Murray also did something else that didn't help his cause. He chose the occasion of a tragedy to lash out at critics of the coal mining industry in general, inviting charges that he was the kind of person who was willing to use a tragic situation to make a political point.

In dealing with the media Murray made an honest effort to present the facts of the situation, at least as he understood them. He clearly demonstrated his willingness to take responsibility and do whatever he possibly could to deal with an increasingly dire situation. But then, for some inexplicable reason, he chose to talk about what mattered to him rather than what mattered to the people with whom he was trying to communicate. The families and friends of the missing miners weren't concerned about the fate of the American coal mining industry, much less the company that owned the Crandall Canyon mine. They didn't care whether Murray and his company were getting a fair shake from union activists or government regulators. They only cared about the fate of those six trapped miners, and later the rescuers who lost their lives trying to save them. By taking his eye off the ball and allowing himself to abandon his strategic objective, Murray opened himself up to a firestorm of criticism from all sides. Pretty soon, his critics were having a field day commenting on his mining methods, past safety violations, and his outspoken opposition to environmental regulation.

It no longer mattered whether Murray's heart was in the right place. It no longer mattered whether he was doing everything humanly possible to rescue the missing miners. His credibility had been destroyed. Murray's willingness to speak his mind began to be perceived as heartless arrogance, and he quickly lost control of the story. Instead of identifying with the concerns of the miners and their families he chose to talk about what mattered to him. As a result, when it came time to deliver the devastating news that the missing miners might never be found, it was easy for grieving families, headline-grabbing politicians, and a host of other critics to blame Murray personally, even though the true cause of the mine collapse was still unknown and there was no credible evidence that he was in any way responsible for the failed rescue. Murray's failure to communicate effectively made him an easy target for anger and blame. Emotional perceptions quickly replaced verifiable facts as the predominating theme of the story.

Tough Times in West Virginia

The same thing can happen even when there is no loss of life. Some years ago Union Carbide owned a large chemical plant in the little town of Institute, West Virginia, where it made a potentially deadly chemical called methyl isocyanate (MIC). The plant was essentially a duplicate of the infamous Union Carbide plant in Bhopal, India, where almost four thousand people died and many thousands more were seriously injured when MIC leaked from a storage tank in 1984. Needless to say, in the wake of the Bhopal disaster, workers at the Institute plant and anyone living nearby were concerned about what could happen if a similar leak were to occur in their backyard.

Several potentially deadly leaks did, in fact, occur at Institute, but they were so quickly controlled that nobody was harmed or ever put in serious danger. Nevertheless, the people of Institute were frightened and outraged. Senior officials of Union Carbide came to Institute to meet with workers and the community and try to allay their fears. Their intentions were good, but their execution left a great deal to be desired. During one infamous community meeting, a meeting still being talked about by Institute workers who were there at the time, a senior Union Carbide official delivered an impassioned speech during which he observed that the company could quite easily solve whatever problems it faced at

Institute by simply closing the plant and walking away. He wasn't trying to threaten or intimidate the community. Quite to the contrary, he was trying to assure anyone listening that Carbide was committed to staying the course and doing everything it could to keep the plant running safely and profitably for everyone's benefit. He tried to illustrate his point by telling a story about a dog he once owned who had a habit of chasing the mailman. But he didn't get too far into his anecdote before he was shouted down by the angry crowd. His heart was in the right place, but he was trying to make his point in exactly the wrong way.

What he wanted the audience to understand was that the company had no intention of abandoning the Institute plant. It wouldn't turn its back on its loyal workforce. It was committed to doing everything possible to operate the Institute plant safely. But the crowd heard something entirely different. All they heard was a big shot from out of town talking about what mattered to him, not what mattered to them. They heard an arrogant company official telling them they weren't smart enough to understand why a Bhopal disaster could never happen in West Virginia. They heard themselves being compared to a rich man's pet dog. The facts may have been on the Union Carbide official's side, but he destroyed his message with careless rhetoric.

The most effective messages not only express concern, but also demonstrate genuine commitment, a sincere promise to do whatever it takes to deal with any problem that might arise. And they reflect your good character and that of the organization you represent. But caring and commitment alone add up to little more than a dull mission statement. Every company has one hanging on the wall, but few ever bother to read it, and nobody can remember who was on the committee that wrote it. As that unfortunate Union Carbide official discovered during his ill-fated visit to West Virginia, concern and commitment are not credible unless they are supported by very specific action. To be effective, a message must convince the audience that you care about the problem in the same way they do, and that you share their concerns and respect their values. To be effective, your message must demonstrate that you and your organization are sincerely committed to doing whatever it takes to solve the problem and make sure it doesn't happen again. But in order to achieve these first two objectives, your message must be supported by specific examples of what you are doing—examples that relate to the target audience, examples they will understand and appreciate, examples that respond to their irrational fears and emotional concerns.

Logos, Ethos, and Pathos

Aristotle summed up this concept by teaching that to be effective a message must pass the three-part test of *logos, ethos,* and *pathos.* In more modern terms, this means that a message must be *true* (logos), it must be *true to you* (ethos), and it must *ring true* to the audience (pathos). Truth, of course, is an absolute prerequisite for any effective message. Your message must be true, period. Not half true, or true some of the time, or true in the eyes of some people but not others. Interpretation is always subjective, but the facts should speak for themselves. Your task as a communicator is to present those facts in a way that will make them not only understandable but also believable and acceptable to the audience.

A good example of how critical the action step can be is the communications and public relations disaster that developed in the immediate aftermath of Hurricane Katrina in 2005. Without getting into the question of who may have been responsible for what did or didn't happen during the hurricane response and recovery, it is useful to look back to what millions were seeing on television in the days following the storm. While government officials were holding live press conferences in Washington to assure victims and the rest of the country that the situation was under control and that help was on the way, they were often joined on the screen by live pictures of dead bodies floating down flooded streets and thousands of desperate refugees descending on the Louisiana Superdome and convention center in New Orleans. No further comment from reporters was necessary. The pictures spoke for themselves, and those pictures immediately and irrevocably destroyed the government's already shaky credibility. There was nothing government officials could do from that point on to convince anyone that what they were seeing on television might not be the whole story.

The government officials conducting those news conferences weren't deliberately lying about what was going on in New Orleans. They were merely telling the truth as they knew it. But the people they were trying to reach could see with their own eyes that the reality of the situation was very different. Under the circumstances, just saying "we care and we're committed" wasn't getting the job done, on the scene or in the minds of the wider audience. For the government's statements to have any credibility at all, those messages about caring and commitment had to be backed up with visible and effective action, such as pictures of relief workers at least appearing to be doing something useful. But those images would not emerge for many days. And by that time the story of the hurricane, the floods, and the horrible aftermath had already been indelibly defined in the public mind by images of unimaginable death and destruction and an almost complete absence of effective government action. The issue had been framed. This was no longer a story about weather. From now on it would be a story about government insensitivity and incompetence. The terms of the discussion had been established, and the government was the villain.

Credibility also depends on the audience's perception of your ethos, your personal character, and your reputation. No matter how articulate you may be, it is tough to deliver a message effectively unless you really believe it and unless your credibility has already been firmly established ahead of time. You cannot deliver a message effectively unless it is *true to you.* Moreover, if your character or credibility have already been called into question for any reason, it will be difficult, if not impossible, to convince an audience to accept what you have to say. Just ask those hapless government officials who are still trying to sell the story of an effective response to the 2005 hurricane even in the face of all that horrible visual evidence to the contrary. Just ask that Union Carbide official who tried to reassure the people of Institute, West Virginia, that they were perfectly safe, even after the disaster at an identical plant in India.

As hard as it may be to accept logically, the truth of your message, and even the personal character and commitment you put behind it, are only a first step. Your message must not only respect the values of the audience and resonate with their emotional concerns, it must also pass the even more difficult test of believability. Your message must *ring true* to the audience you are trying to reach.

We once had a client who was in serious trouble with state regulators. The company had the verifiable facts on its side when it argued that the very consumers those regulators were claiming to protect consistently gave the company 98 percent customer satisfaction ratings. At first we were understandably suspicious of that incredibly favorable satisfaction number. How could any company in any business, especially one that found itself in such serious legal trouble in so many jurisdictions, possibly be meeting the needs and expectations of almost all its customers almost all the time? Needless to say, the regulators were just as suspicious. But our own independent polling confirmed our client's numbers completely. As far as we could determine, this company really did enjoy a legitimate 98 percent customer satisfaction rating. And they were absolutely committed to keeping it that way. Unfortunately, being absolutely true didn't make their message one bit more effective with the audience they needed to reach.

In this particular situation, the audience of greatest immediate concern was made up of those state regulators, few, if any, of whom would ever be in the market for our client's product. Our client's millions of customers were indeed 98 percent satisfied. But that message fell flat with the target audience of suspicious regulators. It didn't matter that our client's message rang true for their customers. It was never likely to ring true with the real target audience. Whatever all those happy customers may have felt about the company, those professionally suspicious, and often politically ambitious, state regulators were convinced that our client was guilty of massive fraud and had to be punished severely. Politicians and activist groups saw bold headlines and big settlement dollars dancing in front of their eyes.

Rather than engage in a futile and expensive debate over the facts, specifically that amazing 98 percent satisfaction score, we counseled our client instead to make peace with the politicians and activists on their terms and then reposition the company as a champion of consumer protection. At last report, our client's customers are still satisfied. But far more important, those politically motivated regulators, having made their headlines and negotiated their multi-million-dollar settlements, are now perfectly happy to point to our client as the gold standard for consumer protection and look elsewhere in the industry for targets. The terms of the debate have changed, at least as far as the company we represented is concerned. Our client's competitors are now fighting their own battles with regulators over whether they should be forced to follow our client's court-imposed consumer protection practices.

Well-respected Washington, D.C., public-relations expert Scott Widmeyer tells a similar story about some message testing his firm, Widmeyer Communications, once did for the Department of Health and Human Services.* The topic was schoolyard bullying. The message the government wanted to get across to kids was that adults would help, if only the kids would ask. But, according to Widmeyer, the nine- to-thirteen-year-olds to whom the message was directed were having none of it. Bitter experience had convinced them that adults, no matter what they might say, really didn't care all that much about bullying, and were therefore unlikely to be of much help in dealing with the problem. Deep down, the kids felt they were on their own, hard facts and the good intentions of adults notwithstanding, HHS needed to find a more credible message if it ever hoped to reach this skeptical target audience. Sometimes just understanding what isn't working and why is half the battle.

Why Qualify?

No matter how powerful and obvious your message may seem to you, the true test of its effectiveness is how long the audience remembers it. A message that isn't remembered is unlikely to be acted upon. One way to make a message more memorable, and

* *Widmeyer Wire,* October 2004.

therefore more effective, is to strip away unnecessary qualification. Sometimes, out of what we perceive to be courtesy, or because of some level of genuine uncertainty, we are tempted to qualify our messages with phrases like *we hope,* or *we believe,* or *we think.* But in the realm of persuasive communication, if something is worth saying at all it is worth saying without qualification. If you are not already convinced that your message can pass the test of absolute truthfulness, you should not be using it in the first place. Unfortunately, speaking without qualification can be difficult in situations where legal or regulatory issues are involved. SEC regulations, for example, impose strict limits on what officials of public companies are allowed to say about financial results and future business prospects. In order to stay within the law, your lawyers may compel you to add some qualification or disclaimer to your messages, but in the interest of making your messages as memorable and effective as possible, you should always try to push the envelope as far as the law allows.

Focusing Your Facts

In order to add credibility and increase interest you should always support your messages with solid evidence. Facts, of course, are the most basic form of support, as long as you are sure those facts will resonate with the target audience. But just as too many cooks can spoil an otherwise delicious stew, too many facts can dilute even the strongest message and make it difficult to remember. It may seem odd that adding too much support can actually weaken a message, but the reason is really very simple. If you are being called upon to talk about an issue, you presumably know a lot about it. And that, ironically, is the first roadblock you face on the path to making your message memorable to the audience you need to reach. It isn't easy to decide from among all the points you might want to make which are really the most important for you to get across to a particular audience at a particular time. It is equally difficult to decide which bits of evidence will best support that message. Faced with such difficult choices, you may be tempted simply to pour out everything you know about the subject, in the desperate hope that something you say will bring someone around to your point of view. But, in fact, the more you say, the less any audience is likely to remember. Strategic communication is often a matter of multiplication by subtraction. The most effective communicators usually focus on a single clear message supported by just a few carefully chosen and well-focused pieces of evidence.

Consider what happened when some market researchers offered shoppers at a gourmet store in California a choice of jams to sample.* When the researchers offered shoppers a choice of thirty different jams, they found that only 3 percent stopped and bought a jar. But when the researchers displayed only six selections, they found that 30 percent of shoppers made a purchase. Giving your audience too many choices and too much to think about at any one time makes it much harder for them to focus on your most important message. As a result, they may just tune out and not remember anything you say. By limiting what the audience has to process at any one time you will correspondingly increase the chances that the most important point you want to make will stick in their minds and have a real impact.

Try this experiment for yourself. Pull ten playing cards from a deck at random and show them one at a time to a friend or col-

---

* Justin Fox, "Why Johnny Can't Save for Retirement," *Fortune,* March 21, 2005, p. 208.

league. Unless your friend has a photographic memory, he probably won't be able to recall more than one or two of the cards you show. Now, repeat the experiment with just one card and see what happens. Your colleague may not remember that single card forever, but he will certainly remember it longer than he would any one card from that original pile of ten. Try the same thing again with a group of people. Not only are none of them likely remember all the cards, but each individual is likely to remember different ones. You have no way of knowing or controlling who remembers what, or whether what they remember is what you think is most important. When trying to convey important information, always try to keep it simple. Never ask your audience to remember too much. Avoid competing with your own key message.

Trouble with Numbers

Supporting a key message with numbers and statistics can be both very helpful and very troublesome, depending on how the numbers are used. For example, astronomer and television personality, Carl Sagan, was famous for looking up into the sky and speaking dramatically about "billions and billions of stars." Sagan never bothered to be specific about just how many billions of stars might actually be twinkling out there in the vast universe. He didn't need to. The point he was trying to make was simply that there are a whole lot of stars in the sky. Far too many to count. As an accomplished communicator, Dr. Sagan understood that big, complicated numbers are much too hard for most people to process, so they just tune them out. In fact, nobody knows exactly how many stars there are in the universe. But even if Dr. Sagan could have cited a precise number, it would have served only to make his message harder to remember. When someone refers to "nine out of ten dentists," most people instantly get the point. They aren't really interested in exactly how many hundreds or thousands of dentists are involved, and they probably wouldn't remember the precise number for very long anyway.

On the other hand, simple and startling statistics, used sparingly, are naturally memorable: "New York City schools enrolled nearly a million students last year, a number roughly equal to the entire population of the state of Nevada." What drives home the point here is the comparison. A million here, a million there, it's a big number, but not very relevant on its own. Only professional public school administrators understand how big a big-city school system really is anyway. Framing the number of public school children in New York City in terms of the population of an entire state, however, makes it easy for ordinary people to understand and remember the meaning and importance of the statistic, even if they can't recall the precise number.

Quoting well-recognized experts can add credibility and interest to a message, but keep in mind that not everyone in your target audience will necessarily agree that a particular expert is actually credible. Moreover, in this skeptical age many people are inclined to assume that every so-called "expert" has a point of view or even a special interest, and they are often correct.

There are a number of other ways you can add a little spice to your messages and make them a lot more memorable:

- **Word Pictures:** To get fresher milk, you'd have to keep a cow in your kitchen.
- **Quotations:** Harry Truman said, "The buck stops here."
- **Metaphors:** We are a top-of-the-line company; you cannot expect us to sell our products at bottom-of-the-barrel prices.

- **Similes:** Our economy is on a course as disastrous as the Titanic!
- **Alliteration:** This is a case of potholes and politics.
- **Pop Culture:** We are as dependable for our clients as Michael Jordan was for the Bulls.
- **Examples:** The O. J. Simpson trial showed how cameras in the courtroom have reshaped the legal landscape.
- **Colorful Action Words:** *Overhaul* instead of *improve*. *Launch* instead of *start*. *Slash* instead of *cut*.
- **Anecdotes:** One day Joe Smith walked into my office with an idea to quadruple production without adding a penny to our costs, switching from flea collars to flea cuffs.
- **Analogies:** Denying tobacco subsidies to North Carolina is like telling Hawaii it cannot grow pineapples. This is like asking us to dance *Swan Lake* wearing skis, and then complaining that we aren't very graceful. Blaming us for what happened here is like punching out the mail carrier for delivering your credit card bill.

Notice that one thing many of these examples have in common is a strong visual element. Most people remember vivid visual images more easily than they remember mere words. They probably will recall a startling visual comparison, such as "the corn is as high as an elephant's eye," even if they aren't all that curious to know just how high off the ground the average elephant's eye happens to be. The point is that the corn is really high, and it is the image of a big elephant standing in the midst of all those towering corn stalks that sticks in the mind. Making your message more visual helps the audience remember what you say.

Another very effective way to make a point is to tell a story. A strong message always has a strong story line, a victim, a villain, a winner, a loser, some kind of conflict, a theme that is easy to grasp. Personal involvement adds even more credibility to a story. Most people relate better to another person than they do to an abstract idea, no matter how important that idea may seem at first glance. The better they relate, the longer they remember. So, whenever possible, try to make your point with a story from your own immediate experience. Supporting your message with a memorable personal story adds an all-important human dimension that brings an otherwise cold and abstract message to life. And always try to speak in simple terms, even to specialized audiences. Avoid jargon and technical language. Big words and fancy technical terms won't really make you look any smarter, but they may very well obscure your message and make it harder for others to remember the point you are trying to make.

Respect the language. Avoid the temptation to use the latest buzz words and catch phrases. Why is every new product, no matter how mundane, now described as some sort of a "system"? Why is the word *solution* so often used as a euphemism for "software"? The idea, I guess, is to make hardworking software salesmen seem both hip and serious at the same time. But in standard English, not every new product can properly be called a system. Software is software and solutions are solutions. Bourbon and water is a solution. Microsoft Office is just a piece of software. A good bourbon and water leaves most users quite satisfied. Even the most expensive and aggressively promoted software often doesn't.

Finding the most effective mix of facts, quotes, and illustrations to support the points you want to make requires careful preparation. It can't be done at the last minute or off the top of your head. If you are willing to take a strategic approach and invest the time to prepare, there are some simple but powerful tools that will help you put into practice the fundamental principles of message development and delivery.

3 /

What's Your Point?

Putting Principles into Practice

eveloping effective strategic messages is an orderly and logical process. But remember, always look at communication from the outside in. Never assume that just because you know a lot about your subject and hold passionately to your point of view that anyone else will automatically embrace it. That's where strategic communication comes into play. By following a step-by-step process, you can refine and focus what you want to say and come up with the most effective way to say it in order to reach any audience in any situation. It doesn't really matter how much time you spend going through these steps. You could spend weeks and months, or just a few minutes. The key is to use whatever time you have available to consider each step carefully and in order.

Strategic Objective

First, ask yourself: What is my *strategic objective?* Before addressing the tactical aspects of message delivery, you must first understand very clearly what you are trying to accomplish at a strategic level. Before you decide what your message will be, you must first understand why you are trying to deliver a message in the first place. If you don't have a point to make, any attempt at communication is likely to be a pointless exercise. The key to successful communication is always to think strategically.

For example, if you are the manager of that exploding chemical plant and find yourself called to the front gate to answer questions from the media, or perhaps even directly from people living in the neighboring community, what is your strategic objective? You will certainly want to provide the latest information about what happened, who was injured, and what your team is doing to deal with the catastrophe. But these are only the immediate tactical considerations. Your larger, strategic objective is really to convince a lot of very worried people that they aren't going to die. Your strategic objective, therefore, is *reassurance.* Your tactical approach is to provide timely, accurate, and credible information. But whatever message delivery tactics you choose must always serve this larger strategic purpose. Strategy defines tactics, never the other way around.

Target Audience

Next, carefully consider your *target audience.* If you seriously expect anyone to pay attention to what you have to say, you shouldn't try to communicate with too many different audiences at the same time. In order to reach your most important target audiences effectively, you must first understand and appreciate exactly who they are demographically and psychologically. For example, in the case of that unlucky chemical plant manager, the audiences of greatest immediate importance probably include the plant's employees, their families, and the neighbors who live nearby. These are the people with the most at stake in the short run. These are the people with the greatest immediate and pressing concerns as flames light up the night and smoke rises into the sky. These are the people with something serious to worry about. Regulators, investors, corporate management, and other constituencies are important, too, of course, but their lives and homes are not in any immediate danger. Their concerns are more abstract, at least for the time being. They can wait. The news media, although usually the first to ask questions, are never themselves a target audience. The media are just a means to an end, a way for you to reach your real target audience more rapidly and efficiently. Educating reporters can be a useful exercise, but only to the extent that it helps those reporters better inform the audiences you need to reach. Bringing a reporter around to your point of view is worthwhile only to the extent that it may encourage that reporter to deliver your message to the target audience.

Emotional Concerns

Once you have clearly identified the specific audience you need to reach, ask yourself what makes those people tick at an emotional level. What the audience already knows and what you want them to know are important, but how the audience *feels* about the issue or situation at hand is far more important to the ultimate effectiveness of your message. In order to reach a particular audience with your message you need to understand and appreciate the emotional concerns that inform their attitudes and motivate their reactions. Don't be tempted to brush aside these emotional issues as unimportant or obvious. Force yourself to make a list of the emotional concerns of your target audience and then consider them carefully. Changing another person's mind is often less a matter of scoring points in a debate over the facts than it is about influencing deeply rooted emotions over the long term.

While the media are never your primary audience, the questions you get from the media are likely to reflect their understanding and appreciation of the interests and concerns of the broader audience. The news media, after all, make their living by serving as surrogates for their readers, viewers, and listeners. Reporters and editors are always looking for stories to which the audience will respond. Reporters are expected to ask the questions that members of the audience would ask if they were doing the interview themselves. Thinking like a reporter is a good way of getting in touch with the concerns of any audience.

Anticipating Questions

At this point you can bring into play another practical message development tool, grouping audience concerns and likely questions into broad categories. Trying to guess precisely every question that you might be asked or that might be on the minds of the audience you need to reach may seem like a necessary exercise, but it is usually just a waste of valuable time. Trying to figure out just how a particular question will be asked is even less efficient. We were firm was once called in to help a client deal with a serious chemical spill in a major harbor. By the time we got involved, the spill was already several days old, but our client had not yet said anything at all to the media or the public. Instead of reaching out to the people they needed to reassure, they were still diligently laboring behind the scenes to complete a question-and-answer document that had already grown to some forty pages, with each and every detailed answer carefully reviewed and dissected by a team of high-priced lawyers.

We looked at the questions and answers just as carefully, but with an entirely different purpose in mind. In order to simplify the process of actually communicating with the public, we sorted all the questions into categories based on our analysis of the concerns of the most important target audiences. We looked at the problem from the outside in, rather than from the inside out. Very quickly we found that all those pages of detailed questions could be grouped into just a few broad areas of concern. Everything else could be set aside as redundant, miscellaneous, or just plain irrelevant. It certainly would be nice to be able to predict every specific question that might be asked and then memorize a bulletproof, legally approved answer that could be delivered on command. But that would require feats of memory far beyond the ability of most people. It is much more efficient to look at potential questions in terms of broad categories, usually no more than four or five in any situation. Then, for each of these four or five categories, you can develop a solid response that is consistent with your larger strategic objective. It is much easier to remember four or five responses to the most strategically significant issues and concerns than it is to memorize forty or fifty pages of tedious questions and answers.

For example, in the case of the exploding chemical plant those workers, families, and neighbors are probably worried about what caused the blaze. Were plant managers negligent? Is the plant a ticking time bomb that poses a constant danger to the surrounding community? They will probably wonder about the potential long-term environmental impact of the accident. Will their health or that of their children be at risk? They might be worried about the economic implications of the incident. Will the plant be forced to close? For how long? Are their jobs at risk? What about the economic health of the community? Just about any imaginable question that might be raised about this particular event, at least initially, will probably fall into one of these broad categories. Don't bother trying to guess which questions will be asked or how they will be framed. Keep your eye on the big picture.

What to Avoid

Next, ask yourself what questions you must for some reason avoid answering. Then consider carefully how you plan to do it. There is, of course, no magic formula that will keep tough questions from being asked. And there is no reason to avoid answering a question just because it happens to be difficult. Considering the hardest questions that could possibly arise is a necessary part of preparing for any communications encounter. In any situation there will almost certainly be questions that you are sure you will be asked, but which for some good reason you must avoid answering. The challenge is doing so without destroying your credibility.

There is a remarkably simple and straightforward way to do this, even under the most challenging circumstances. As always, tell the truth. Don't allow yourself to slip into denial. Anticipate the questions that will fall into this troublesome category and be prepared to explain exactly why you cannot answer them. For example, if the question concerns a matter in litigation, refer the questioner to the lawyers. If the question involves a confidential personnel matter, explain that company policy, not to mention federal law, prevents you from discussing it. If answering the question would require you to reveal proprietary business information, politely explain that you would certainly like to answer, but since your competitors would also like to have the information, you will have to decline. Your objective is to be seen not as someone trying to hide information, but rather as someone trying to be helpful to the best of your ability. Brushing off a reasonable question by saying something like "I can't go there" or "I won't talk about that" leaves the impression that you are trying to hide something important and perhaps embarrassing. Explaining in simple terms why you can't answer the question preserves your credibility without compromising your organization.

Former AT&T corporate communications chief Dick Martin was on to something very important when he pointed out that the real goal of strategic communication is not media coverage. Rather, it is credibility, that most valuable and fragile communications asset that any individual or organization can possess.* Without a good reputation, a positive image, a reservoir of credibility, it is very difficult to convince others to listen to you, believe what you say, or act on it. Reputation and credibility are hard to win and easy to lose. Failing to acknowledge and respond to specific questions and legitimate concerns, even if you are unable to provide answers as detailed as the questioner would like, can seriously damage your credibility, even if you sincerely believe that the questions you are being asked are irrelevant, inappropriate, or just plain stupid. Answering specific questions is always just a means to an end, the point at which the serious communication process

---

* Dick Martin, *Tough Calls: AT&T and the Hard Lessons Learned from the Telecom Wars* (New York: AMACOM/American Management Association, 2005).

begins, not where it ends. Merely answering questions is never your ultimate strategic purpose. But you must always be prepared to address the questions you are asked or risk sending a clear and convincing message that you don't care or, worse, have something to hide.

While every question deserves polite acknowledgment, you should never feel obligated to answer a question just because it is asked. If you don't know the answer to a particular question, just say, "I don't know," or refer the questioner to a more appropriate source. No matter how hard you may be pressed, never let yourself be tempted to speculate. Never try to answer "what if?" hypothetical questions. Stick with what you know to be absolutely true. When faced with the temptation to speculate it is wise to recall Abraham Lincoln's observation that it is better to keep your mouth shut and be thought a fool than to speak up and remove all doubt. Credibility is too precious to risk with careless and unnecessary speculation.

Key Message

Finally, step back and ask yourself what is the one *key message* you want to get across no matter what? What is the story you want to tell? What is the point you want to make, and how will making that point further the strategic objective you identified at the beginning of the message development process? This last question is particularly important, and very easy to overlook. Just because you happen to feel comfortable with a certain message, or sound good saying it, doesn't guarantee that it is really the most strategically important point you need to make. Because messaging is a strategic exercise, your key message must always be the one that most effectively advances your strategic objective.

Message Development Checklist

Keep this summary checklist handy whenever you are working through the message development process:

- What is your *strategic objective?*
- Who is your *target audience?*
- What are they *concerned* about?
- How will you *respond* to those concerns?
- What areas do you need to *avoid?*
- What is your *key message?*
- Does your key message advance your strategic objective?

Message Pyramid

Another very powerful message delivery tool for message preparation is the *message pyramid.* Once you have settled on your responses to the concerns of your target audience and chosen the one key message you want that audience to remember, using the message pyramid will help you shape and structure what you say for maximum impact and recall.

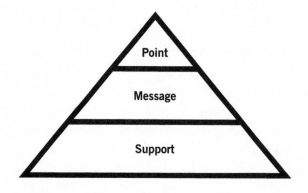

The message pyramid is useful precisely because it contradicts the way most of us are naturally inclined to answer a question or make a point. Most of us have been trained since childhood to argue from the available evidence, what we know or believe about something, to a specific conclusion, the point we want to make. That's the way a legal brief is structured. That's the way a budget memo is written. That's the way a joke is told. The punch line is always saved for the end. In other words, we naturally put the message we want to deliver at the bottom of the pyramid. This may seem logical, but it is actually a very inefficient way to make a point to a distracted and skeptical audience. Experience has shown that it is almost always more effective to start with the point you want to make (delivered as a memorable summary statement, quote, or sound bite), followed by the message itself, followed finally by carefully selected supporting evidence and examples.

The short statement at the top of the pyramid helps to grab the audience's attention and makes them keep paying attention long enough for you to deliver the message itself. The top of the pyramid need not be a clever sound bite or "bumper sticker" statement. It might be nothing more than a simple summary of the main point you want to make. But whatever you say first should quickly and clearly make your point to the audience and make them appreciate why it is important to keep listening to the rest of what you are about to say. The supporting evidence is saved for last, so that by the time you get down to the details your listener will already have a good idea of what those points of supporting evidence mean and why they matter. If you begin by immediately flooding your audience with evidence and examples, no matter how relevant or interesting they may be, your listeners probably will have stopped paying attention long before you finally get to the point you want to make. If they are still listening at all, they are sure to wonder how the intriguing point you just made relates to all that other stuff you've been saying. You need to make your point clearly right at the beginning if you expect anyone to pay attention long enough to listen to the rest of the story.

The message pyramid forces you to think carefully in advance about exactly what you want to say and how you want to say it. It forces you to focus on the point you want to make and how to make that point as interesting and important to the audience as it already is to you. The pyramid forces you to explain clearly why what you are about to say is important, even before you actually say it. Perhaps most important, the message pyramid forces you to decide which pieces of supporting evidence will be most effective at bringing your message to life and making it believable. Burdening the audience with too much evidence increases the chances that they will remember the wrong things, or nothing at all. One or two bits of memorable supporting evidence will make your message effective. Offering too much evidence risks making it too easily forgettable.

Some examples of how the message pyramid works in practice:

Opening Statement: Your peace of mind is our most important product.

Key Message: In order to make sure that our widgets are the safest and most reliable you can buy anywhere, we have developed the most advanced testing program in our industry.

Supporting Evidence: Last year, for example, we spent over $10 million safety testing every widget that left this plant. Just last week I spent a day in the factory myself, checking out the testing procedures. My family uses our widgets every day, and I want to see for myself that they are safe.

Opening Statement: There are three reasons why this quarter has been difficult for the company: foreign competition, internal restructuring, and steadily increasing labor costs.

Key Message: Competition from overseas has never been more intense. Foreign companies are able to make widgets at a fraction of what it costs us to make them. We knew going in that our company-wide restructuring program would be costly and disruptive in the short run, but we also know that it will pay big dividends down the line, in part because it will bring our labor costs more in line with those of our overseas competitors.

Supporting Evidence: Last year alone, our main competitor in South Korea increased its widget sales by 300 percent. That's fifty million more widgets than they were able to sell the year before. And, while we have cut our cost of making widgets by nearly 40 percent, thanks to plant closures and other restructuring efforts, our labor costs are still uncompetitive, about three cents per widget compared with only about a penny for our Korean competitors.

The top of the pyramid doesn't have to be a clever sound bite, but summing up the point you want to make with a memorable quote can make it a lot more effective. Once, when I was called upon to discuss the issue of campaign finance reform on the *Today* show, I had an opportunity to put this principle into practice. The question was whether the government should require radio and television stations to give political candidates free advertising time. Supporters of the idea argued that giving candidates free air time would help make elections more honest by making money less important in campaigns. Opponents of the idea, myself included, argued that candidates would just use the free time and then keep right on raising money to buy even more time. Knowing that I would have only a short time to make my point, I spent several days trying to come up with a sound bite that would make my message memorable for the audience. I finally settled on an analogy. When my turn came I suggested that trying to make a politician honest by giving him free air time was like trying to reform a bank robber by giving him a free ATM card. The supporter of free air time who appeared with me on the broadcast stuck to his philosophical arguments. But I made my point in a way the audience couldn't help but remember. I used the message pyramid. Who do you think won the debate?

Bridging

If you have paid attention to the concerns of the audience, you will be able to predict fairly accurately the general areas of questioning you will face in most communications situations. If you have done your homework, you will be ready with accurate, credible, and well-structured responses that address the four or five broad lines of questioning you anticipate. But your most important objective is not just to answer specific questions. It is to deliver your key message and make your point, and there is a simple but powerful technique called "bridging" that you can use to make a smooth transition from response to message.

If you are lucky enough to be asked a specific question that just happens to be directly related to your message, the process is relatively simple. You just answer with your message and then wait for the next question. You have made your point and you don't need to go any further. But in most situations, the specific questions you will be asked are more likely to be about topics not necessarily related directly to your key message, so you will have to work just a little bit harder to bridge from your response over to your message.

For example, suppose the key message you want to deliver is about your company's long-term business development plans, but the first question you get is about the overall state of the Asian economy. Since you do a lot of business in Asia, questions about the Asian economy should be expected, and you should be prepared to address them. But in order to make the discussion serve your strategic objective you must do more than just answer the specific questions you are asked. You need to build a bridge that will carry you from the answers you have prepared for predictable questions over to the main point you want to make.

> **Question:** What do you think will be the near-term effects of the problems with the Asian economy?
>
> **Answer:** The effects of Asia's economic problems are likely to be minimal, as long as the rest of the world economy remains steady.
>
> **Bridge:** But what's more important to realize . . .
>
> **Key Message:** . . . is that here in America, our company is committed to long-term product development in some very exciting new technologies. For example, we have very promising research underway that will eventually lead to cheaper and more powerful microchips.

This seems simple enough, but most of us are so accustomed to answering each and every question promptly and accurately and then waiting politely to be asked another that we completely forget to bridge, even when we have a well-developed strategic message all ready to deliver.

Bridging may not come naturally to most people, but it really isn't all that complicated. The simplest bridge words of all are *and* and *but.* As you practice your responses to anticipated questions, you can also try using other bridging phrases. To make a smooth transition over to the key message you want the audience to remember:

What's really important here is . . .
What I'd really like you to remember is . . .
I appreciate your concern, but I'd like to offer another
    perspective . . .
Let's look at the big picture for a moment . . .
Looked at in this way . . .
The real issue here is . . .
Let's put that in context . . .
You make a good point, however . . .
The bottom line is . . .
Taking a broader look . . .
I might frame that question a bit differently . . .

Politicians often skip this bridging step entirely and just deliver their canned message over and over again, regardless of whatever specific question they may have been asked. But you can't afford to sound like a politician. In order to protect your credibility you must be careful to acknowledge and address the direct questions that are put to you. Then, after answering the question, you must have the discipline to bridge to the point you want to make. Think of your answers to specific questions as the price you pay to play the game. Successful delivery of your strategic message is the prize you are playing to win.

What if things get ugly? What if you are suddenly asked a hostile question, or one based on a clearly false premise? Never allow yourself to be put on the defensive. When faced with a false premise question like, "Isn't it true that your company decided several years ago to ignore safety problems at this plant because you are planning to close it anyway?" you can say something like, "That's not true," or "I would never characterize it that way," or just, "No," and then follow immediately with what *is* true, your key message, the story you want to tell, the way you want to tell it.

Implication of the Opposite

When denying a false premise it is very tempting to repeat it. But that is always a big mistake. Aristotle called this error the "implication of the opposite." Most of us probably are more familiar with it in terms of President Richard Nixon's now infamous statement in response to a newspaper editor's question: "I am not a crook." Unfortunately for Mr. Nixon and his presidency, most of those who heard him make that statement back in 1973 took it to mean that he was, in fact, a crook. He appeared to be an embarrassed and guilty crook trying desperately to cover up his crimes. "I am not a crook" instantly became an enduring symbol of the entire Watergate scandal.

But consider for a moment just what Mr. Nixon actually said in response to what was really a relatively benign question about Florida real estate taxes. He didn't say, "I *am* a crook." He didn't say, "I used to be a crook, but I've since reformed." He didn't say, "Okay guys, I admit I'm a little bit crooked, but Johnson was a whole lot worse." All he said was, "I am not a crook." But by carelessly including the negative word *crook* in his answer, President Nixon unintentionally implied exactly the opposite and instantly put himself on the defensive. He put himself in a position where his enemies could use his own poorly chosen words against him. Repeating the negative makes you look defensive. If you allow yourself to look defensive, people will assume you have something to be defensive about, no matter how straightforward and accurate the substance of your actual statement may be. When it came to the minor real estate transaction to which Mr. Nixon was referring in his answer, there probably was nothing crooked involved at all. But that's not how the statement was perceived by the audience Mr. Nixon was trying to reach. He resigned the presidency nine months later.

Message Testing

As sensitive as we may be to the concerns of our audience, and as clever as we may think we are at coming up with catchy messages to make our case, objective testing will always make a message stronger and help avoid costly tactical errors. No matter how good your gut may be, testing your strategy and your messages with real people, people as much like those you are trying to reach as possible, is good insurance.

There are three basic research tools you can use to test your messages and make sure they are working as well as you anticipate: quantitative opinion research (public opinion polls), focus groups and targeted interviews, and media content analysis. Of the three, opinion polls are the most familiar, and the most often criticized. But carefully designed questions put to a well-constructed population sample will yield a remarkably accurate picture of overall public opinion, including selected demographic subsets of the general population. Polls alone, however, are not sufficient to evaluate the effectiveness of a message, or the unexpected risks that delivering that message might present. Knowing that a particular message works or doesn't work for a particular audience is important, but it is far more important in the long run to understand why, and that's where focus groups come in.

We once worked with a client in the pharmaceutical industry that needed to find an effective way of explaining to the general public that trace amounts of prescription medicines finding their way into the water supply are harmless. Scientists routinely describe these tiny amounts in terms of "parts per million" or "parts per billion," with parts per billion obviously being much smaller. Scientists, of course, understand and appreciate the enormous difference between parts per *million* and parts per *billion*. But the rest of us usually just tune out when we hear terms like this. We all understand that both parts per million and parts per billion describe things that are very small, but very few of us appreciate the magnitude of the difference between the two. In this case, the audience our client was trying reach was not made up of scientists who are comfortable with numbers, big or small. It was made up of ordinary people with every-day, nonscientific doubts and fears. That prescription drug residue ending up in the water supply is potentially dangerous was never in question. The only issue was how to explain how much is too much. The audience understood the concept of small, of course, but we needed to help them appreciate that what our client considered small and harmless was small and harmless enough not to be a threat to public health.

In this case, rather than counting on our skeptical audience to appreciate the technical concept of *parts per billion,* we came up with a simple, and we thought, powerful analogy. By our calculations, the amount of chemical residue from our client's products that ended up in the water supply was roughly the same as an aspirin tablet dissolved in an Olympic size swimming pool. In other words, incredibly small and not worth worrying about. When we tested this and other messages in a focus group, however, the results were a big surprise. Twelve ordinary people chosen more or less at random reacted very negatively to the aspirin tablet analogy. As they explained during the subsequent discussion, aspirin, while a familiar substance and hardly threatening to most people, is nevertheless understood to be a medicine, a drug, something very similar in their minds to what our client was accused of releasing into the environment. To the people in this focus group, using an aspirin tablet to illustrate our point only served to rekindle an intuitive, albeit irrational, fear of any unknown and unwanted medicinal substance finding its way into the water supply. Relating the residue from prescription medicines to another drug, however familiar and benign, served only to remind the members of this focus group of the underlying problem we were trying to address and the emotional concerns we were trying to mitigate.

This focus group reminded us that however clever we may have thought our aspirin tablet analogy was, ordinary people just don't like the idea that they might be swallowing someone else's medicine every time they take a drink of water. When we dropped the aspirin analogy and changed the comparison to a single tiny cube of sugar dissolved in the great big swimming pool we found that the focus group's reaction changed completely. The sugar cube analogy effectively illustrated just how tiny the amounts of medicine reaching the water supply really were, without reminding the audience of anything that worried them.

Using public opinion surveys to test and fine-tune messages works the same way. For any issue in any situation there probably will be a number of messages that you might consider delivering.

Choosing which to use based on how you or your colleagues react is dangerous. You are just too close to the issue. You know too much, and the more you know the harder it is for you to appreciate the concerns of those who know less than you do. Your concerns and priorities are probably very different from those of the people you are trying to reach. Just because you really like a particular message and feel comfortable delivering it doesn't mean that the audience will react the same way. It is much safer and more reliable to use opinion surveys and focus groups to test a variety of different messages and pieces of supporting evidence. Then go public with only those that prove most effective at moving opinion in your direction. This is usually done by posing relevant questions at the beginning of a survey interview in order to establish a baseline of understanding and opinion, then exposing the respondent to your key messages in the course of further questioning, and then posing the same questions again at the end of the interview in order to measure any change in reaction. This kind of message testing helps you understand what your target audience already thinks, feels, and knows, and then lets you measure quite accurately whether what you plan to say will change their minds.

The third basic message-testing tool is media content analysis, tracking how your messages are playing in the media in order to compare the coverage with any change in audience opinion. Is anything the audience is hearing from you, or from the other side, having an impact, positive or negative, weak or strong? This kind of media analysis involves a lot more than just counting how many stories dealing with your issue or quoting your key message were published or broadcast. Sophisticated media analysis measures not only the number of stories, but also the tone of the coverage and the broader context in which the media are telling your story to the public. As the diesel coalition example illustrates, negative media coverage does not automatically move public opinion in a negative direction. But the media do reflect, and to a degree influence, the overall opinion environment. In order to refine your messaging over time it is useful to track both the coverage itself and the impact of that coverage on the ebb and flow of public opinion.

Public Opinion

One reason most media coverage doesn't automatically drive public opinion is that opinions about most issues usually fall across a fairly wide spectrum. At one extreme are your natural supporters, those who will agree with your point of view no matter what, and who are unlikely ever to change their opinion for any reason. At the other end of the spectrum are those who vehemently disagree with you and are unlikely ever to be convinced otherwise. In between are those who may be somewhat predisposed to agree with you, but who might change their minds if your opponents in the debate make a good case, and those who are inclined to disagree with you but might change their minds if you make a better case. Right in the middle are those who have no strong opinion one way or the other and are therefore equally open to persuasion from either side. When it comes to most issues, most of the people you want to reach are comfortably parked squarely in this large middle ground, knowing very little and caring even less.

Unfortunately, most of us are tempted to invest the bulk of our time and energy either delivering our message to those already firmly convinced of our point of view or trying with all our might to win over those who will never change their minds no matter what we say to them. But on most issues, the distribution of public opinion in the real world almost always describes a bell curve. The vast majority of the audience occupies the middle ground.

They may not know or care much about the issue, but they are usually willing to listen, and they are probably open to persuasion. They are the people to whom a smart communicator pays the most attention. Ignore the extremes. Target your message to the genuinely undecided.

4 /

Preparing Powerful Presentations

Making Your Point in Person

Whether it is making a presentation to a small group of colleagues or delivering a formal address to a thousand people, public speaking is for many people a frightening challenge. But today most of us have little choice. Our success in just about any aspect of our personal and professional lives often depends on how effectively we are able to make a point to other people.

Communicating effectively with a live audience requires both a clear and convincing message and a strong physical delivery. As with any other communications opportunity, preparation and practice are the keys to success. Efficient preparation includes focusing on strategic objectives, analyzing target audiences, and framing key messages. But effective delivery to a live audience also demands carefully practiced physical skills such as eye contact, posture, gesture, and the proper use of appropriate visual aids. An effective presentation must be both well structured and well delivered.

A polished delivery won't save a speech that lacks meaningful content, but even the most powerful message can easily get lost if the person trying to deliver it fails to connect with the audience. No matter what the circumstances, you need to feel you know what you want to say and why, you need to feel confident in your ability to deliver your message, and you need to feel you know how to connect with your audience physically and emotionally. Your irrational fear of public speaking will be replaced by a powerful ability to reach any audience, no matter how large or small, and to do it consistently.

Audiences almost always have a short attention span, so you cannot afford to leave any aspect of your message or your delivery to chance. From start to finish you will be competing for attention with all sorts of distractions, many of which you can never hope to control. No matter how simple or safe a particular presentation may seem, failing to prepare is preparing to fail. Investing the time it takes to create a compelling presentation and then paying close attention to every detail of how you deliver it will help ensure that your audience will remember what you say and respond to it positively. Making your point and making sure the audience remembers it are always your most important objectives.

Physical Stress

If you feel uncomfortable standing up to speak in front of a big crowd, or even a small group, or just your boss, you are certainly not alone. Some people are afraid of heights or deep water. But of all the many things that make people uncomfortable, by far the most common is public speaking. In fact, a surprising number of otherwise entirely rational people will freely admit to being more afraid of speaking in public than they are of death. Strange as it may seem, they apparently would prefer being the silent guest of honor at a funeral than the live speaker who has been asked to stand up and deliver the eulogy.

This kind of paralyzing stage fright is obviously unproductive, but a little bit of nervousness before starting to speak to an important audience is perfectly normal and can even be somewhat beneficial. Natural adrenaline is the high-octane fuel you need to energize your presentation. A little nervousness helps keep you alert and focused. Energy, alertness, and focus help to bring a presentation to life. A speaker who is completely calm before an important presentation will probably appear to the audience to be somewhat flat and disinterested. A little nervousness, properly channeled, can help bring out the passion that can turn an otherwise forgettable presentation into something the audience will remember and respond to.

There are a few simple things you can do before any speech or presentation to help manage the purely physical nervousness you feel before taking the stage. Take a few deep breaths. Getting oxygen into your body helps calm you down and loosens up your vocal cords. Do some head and shoulder rolls and stretch your arms above your head. This helps relax your entire body and is especially helpful in loosening up tense muscles in your upper body and neck. Silently run through your message. Don't try to rehearse your entire presentation, just take a moment to be sure the main points you want to make are absolutely clear in your mind. This will help focus your attention and keep your mind free of distractions. And don't forget to smile. It makes you look and feel a lot more positive and confident.

Setting Your Objective

Following the message development formula outlined earlier, your first step in preparing an effective presentation should always be to identify a clear and specific strategic objective. Ask yourself why you are speaking to this audience in the first place. Talking just for the sake of talking is rarely worth the time and trouble. If you don't have an important point to make and a clear strategic reason for making it, you will probably have a tough time getting the audience to pay attention and respond. Ask yourself what you want this particular group of people to remember after you have left the stage. How do you want them to feel? How do you want them to perceive you personally? Above all, what do you want them to *do* as a direct result of what you are about to tell them?

Understanding Your Audience

The most effective way to reach and influence other people is to first demonstrate that you appreciate and sincerely empathize with their values and emotional concerns. Before you start to organize the substance of your presentation, take a moment to think about the audience you will be facing. Who are they? How well do they know who you are? What do they think of you? Are they old or young, liberal or conservative? Where do they come from? What do they care about? What keeps them up at night worrying? What makes them mad? What makes them sad? What makes them glad? Do they already have an opinion about the subject you will be addressing? How well do they understand the issues involved? What are they expecting from you? Why are they there? The better you understand and appreciate the emotions of the people you are trying to reach, the easier it will be for you to answer the two most important questions they will have about what you plan to say: What's in this for me? And why should I bother giving you my time and attention?

In most situations, getting an audience to remember what you say is even harder than getting them to pay attention to your presentation in the first place. You may think your message is critically important, and it may indeed be critically important to you. But even the most attentive and sympathetic audience probably won't remember very much of what you say, and then not for very long. Indeed, barely a half hour after even the most compelling speech or presentation most people in the audience are likely to remember only about 60 percent of what you say. When they get home that night they will probably recall less than half. A week later, if you're lucky, they will remember only about 10 percent of what you have worked so hard to tell them.

Don't take it personally. This is merely a matter of human nature and our society's steadily shrinking attention span. There is nothing you can do about it except to make sure that the audience remembers the *right* 10 percent of what you say. If you try to say too much in any one presentation, the audience will remember very little. Worse, what they do recall may not be what you think is really most important. On the other hand, simple arithmetic suggests that if you focus on a single clear message that effectively advances your strategic objective, you will significantly improve the odds that the audience will remember what you say and act on it. Nothing can absolutely guarantee that they will remember anything, of course, but focusing on a single, powerful message shortens the odds to no worse than fifty-fifty. That's certainly better than trying to make five or ten points and then hoping the audience will somehow remember the one you believe is really most important. Even if you can't control what the audience remembers, you certainly can control what you say, and saying less always helps the audience remember more.

Concerns and Questions

Once you have your strategic objective clearly in mind and have considered carefully how you plan to relate it to the concerns of the audience you are trying to reach, it is time to anticipate their questions. This is more than just a matter of preparing for a possible question-and-answer session at the end of your talk. Just because a particular issue isn't on the formal meeting agenda or doesn't happen to come up during the question and answer session doesn't mean it isn't on the minds of those in the audience. Often what isn't said matters a lot more to them than what is. So discipline yourself to anticipate the toughest questions you could possibly face and think carefully about how you would answer them if given the opportunity. If possible, try to get a step ahead by addressing those questions and concerns during the presentation itself. This is just another way of keeping your message focused on the audience, what they care about, what they expect, and what they will respond to. Addressing their unspoken concerns will help you make your main point more effectively. Decide what you want to say about each of the broad categories of audience interest and concern you have identified. Outline your responses. Gather supporting facts. Choose illustrations that support the points you want to make. When you are comfortable that you have all the categories covered, list your points in order of importance.

Focus

Next consider what you *do not* want to say. Avoid cluttering your presentation with too many points and too many examples. Eliminate any extraneous material that might distract from your key message. An unnecessarily long speech or presentation can easily cause both you and your audience to lose focus and drift away. While there is no strict rule for how long an effective speech or presentation should be, keep in mind that the length of time you actually speak is far less important than the length of time you are able to hold the audience's attention. The ideal speech should last just long enough to make your point and not one second longer. In almost any situation, shorter is usually better.

An equally important aspect of knowing what *not* to say is considering in advance what you cannot discuss, no matter how forcefully you may be questioned. Just because you can't talk about something for some reason doesn't mean the audience doesn't care about it or won't ask you to discuss it if they get the chance. If you simply ignore a subject of obvious concern to the audience, or refuse without a credible explanation to answer questions about it, you will be sending a strong message that you have something to hide. If there is an elephant in the parlor, it is always better to address it on your terms, rather than ignore it and leave yourself open to the suspicion that you are insulting the audience's intelligence by deliberately trying to evade the obvious.

When choosing examples, illustrations, and other forms of support for your key points, avoid material that is so controversial that it might overshadow your primary message. There is nothing wrong with stirring the emotions of your audience, but you never want an example to grab so much attention on its own that it overshadows the message it is intended to support. Always be alert for possible audience sensitivity to matters of politics, race, sex, and religion. In most cases it is best to avoid them altogether. And always try to avoid anything negative. Keep in mind that the most effective messages, even in the most controversial situations, are always positive and proactive, never negative or defensive.

Once you feel you have identified the topics that matter most to the audience, it is time to focus on the one message that matters most to you. This is the main point you want to make, the main thing you want the audience to remember, the top priority on the list of key points you assembled earlier. Make use of the message pyramid to help sharpen and focus the point you want to make. Develop a sparkling, memorable quote that summarizes your message. Then think hard about how you can relate that message to any other topics you know will be of concern to the audience. You don't have to be asked a specific question in order to bridge to your key message.

Organization

It is often helpful to write out a speech or presentation word for word in order to organize the material thoroughly and thoughtfully. When you actually stand up on stage and face the audience, however, you should always try to avoid reading a verbatim text. If you know your material thoroughly, all you really need to have on hand are the barest of notes. A few key words in outline format should be enough to jog your memory and keep you from wandering too far away from your main point. Your ultimate goal in any speech or presentation is carefully planned spontaneity. Having written notes handy will serve as a security blanket and help keep you from getting nervous about losing your train of thought.

One of the most familiar rules of the orator's craft states that you should tell them what you are going to tell them, tell them, and then tell them again what you just told them. With that in mind, try preparing your presentation backward. Draft your conclusion first. This will be your key message, your recommendation, your proposal, your solution, your call to action, your response to the most pressing concerns of the audience, the big point you want to make. This is where you will tell the audience what you want them to remember and what you want them to do when your presentation is over. Framing your conclusion first forces you to sharpen your main point and helps you maintain focus.

Next, tackle the middle. This is where you add the more detailed material that supports your main point. This is where you address other categories of audience concern and relate them back to your key message. But be careful not to burden your presentation with too many digressions or too much supporting evidence. The more material you offer, the harder it will be for the audience to sort out what's really most important.

Finally, write the beginning. The beginning of your speech or presentation should mirror the end, clearly stating your key point even before you explain it or offer any evidence to support it. Many presenters still ignore the message pyramid and insist on organizing their speeches just as they would draft a budget memo or a legal brief. They begin with a mass of evidence and examples and then carefully reason down to a defensible conclusion. But in today's short-attention-span environment the audience has to hear your key message right at the beginning or they won't be able to make much sense of the supporting evidence that follows. Even worse, they probably will have stopped paying attention long before you finally get around to making your main point. Life is unfair. Unless you give the audience a good reason to keep listening, they probably won't.

One way to capture the audience's attention right at the beginning is with *grabbers,* verbal hooks that jump out and force people to pay attention. These could be personal anecdotes, memorable analogies, attention-grabbing illustrations, or dramatic statements.

For example, the legendary architect Frank Lloyd Wright once began a speech in Pittsburgh by calling it "the ugliest city I've ever seen." Who knows whether Wright really had such deep artistic disdain for the Pittsburgh skyline, but he clearly used the line to grab and hold the audience's attention for a talk about the city's architectural heritage. The good citizens of Pittsburgh may not have appreciated what Wright had to say about their buildings, but you can bet they paid close attention to the rest of his talk. Physical props are another good way to dramatize a key point. For example, a teacher once opened a lecture by holding up an apple and trying to peel it with a spoon. A powerful visual image illustrating what can happen if you try to use the wrong tool for the job. The visual image of trying unsuccessfully to peel the apple was much more powerful than any words the teacher may actually have spoken.

Most people remember best what they hear first, what they hear last, and what they hear repeated most often. Communications experts call this the principle of *primacy*, *recency*, and *repetition*. So always be sure to make your main point as powerfully as you possibly can right at the beginning and again at the very end of your presentation. And never be afraid to repeat your main point frequently throughout. Remind the audience over and over again how everything you say relates to the message you want them to remember. Repetition may be tedious on the printed page, but it is the very essence of effective public speaking.

Writing for the Ear

Speeches and presentations are intended to be heard with the ear, not read with the eye. The audience will never see your text or written notes. All they will see is you and whatever visual aids you decide to use. So, as you prepare your copy, force yourself to read it out loud. The best broadcast writers do this routinely. They want to make absolutely sure that what looks good on paper or sounds fine when read silently will still make sense when it is spoken aloud to the audience. If you can't read your copy aloud to yourself smoothly and comfortably, it is highly unlikely that you will be able to deliver it effectively when it comes time to stand up in front of a live audience.

As an example of the difference between writing for the ear and writing for the eye, consider how the following paragraph from a wire service news story written to be read silently from the printed page might be rewritten to be read aloud to a live audience:

**Original written text from
the Associated Press (1/31/06)**

Samuel Anthony Alito Jr. became the nation's 110th Supreme Court justice on Tuesday, confirmed with one of the most partisan victories in modern history after a fierce battle over the future direction of the high court. Alito was sworn in shortly after the vote.

The Senate voted 58–42 to confirm Alito, a former federal appellate judge, U.S. attorney, and conservative lawyer for the Reagan administration from New Jersey, as the replacement for retiring Justice Sandra Day O'Connor, who has been a moderate swing vote on the court.

All but one of the Senate's majority Republicans voted for his confirmation, while all but four of the Democrats voted against Alito.

Rewritten to be read aloud

Samuel Alito has been confirmed as the nation's 110th Supreme Court justice.

Alito was confirmed by the full Senate on Tuesday morning.

The vote was fifty-eight to forty-two.

Alito's confirmation came after a fierce partisan battle over the future of the Supreme Court.

Alito replaces retiring Justice Sandra Day O'Connor.

Justice O'Connor has long been a moderate swing vote on the Supreme Court.

Alito is a former federal appellate judge.

Alito has also served as a U.S. Attorney in his home state of New Jersey and conservative lawyer in the Reagan Administration.

All but one of the Senate's Republican majority voted for Alito's confirmation. All but four Democrats voted against Alito.

Alito was sworn in shortly after the vote.

The same essential information is included in both versions. But the version intended to be read aloud uses simple, declarative sentences and avoids pronouns. It looks a bit strange on the printed page. But it sounds far more natural than the original wire copy when read aloud.

When writing for the ear it is always best to keep your sentences short. Simple, declarative sentences may look choppy in print, but they are the most effective way to make important points to a live audience. Use the active voice whenever possible. Avoid pronouns. On the printed page pronouns are a good substitute for the tedious repetition of proper names. But listeners to a live presentation don't have the luxury of stopping whenever they wish and going back to check an antecedent. They can't be expected to remember all the proper names that your pronouns represent. It is all too easy for them to lose track of your train of thought.

Repetition for emphasis has always been one of the most powerful tools of persuasive oratory. Think back to Dr. Martin Luther King's legendary "I have a dream" speech. Dr. King repeated that key phrase over and over again, emphasizing and reemphasizing his key message, making it easy to remember and impossible to forget. Dr. King wanted us remember his dream, and a half century later we still do. Truly memorable speeches like "I have a dream" also teach another important lesson. Great public speaking is more about poetry than prose. Great speakers always pay close attention to the music of their words and the rhythm of their delivery. They care about how they sound. Simply reading a text, no matter how well written, will sound to the audience like exactly what it is, reading written words out loud. Reciting a text is a far cry from really *delivering* a speech or presentation in a way that will make a live audience remember what you have said and respond to the point you want to make.

Once during a high-level military briefing, former British Prime Minister Margaret Thatcher is reported to have stopped one of her generals just a few seconds into his formal presentation with a simple question. "Are you reading that?" the prime minister asked. When the general replied that indeed he was, Mrs. Thatcher abruptly asked him to hand over the paper. In her typically brisk fashion, Mrs. Thatcher was making it quite clear that she could read the written report much faster all by herself. Unless the general's body language and style of presentation was adding anything important to his presentation, he was wasting the prime minister's valuable time by forcing her to listen while he read his report aloud.

One way to polish the rough spots in your copy is to use what's called a *table read*. Sit down across a table with another person and read through your draft copy line by line. If you stumble on a phrase, try it again. Ask yourself why you had trouble saying the line. If necessary, change the wording to something you can deliver smoothly and easily time after time. Listen carefully to the way you naturally emphasize words and phrases and make note in your script of what you want to emphasize and where you want to pause. Make sure the person to whom you are reading is clearly understanding everything you say and responding as you anticipate. Just because you understand a particular phrase and can deliver it smoothly doesn't mean anyone else will automatically get the point you are trying to make.

Stories and Pictures

Tell stories and be visual. It is much easier for most people to remember and relate to visual images than to abstract concepts. Remember Aesop and his fables. When Aesop wanted to make the abstract concept "slow and steady wins the race" memorable for his audience, he created the now famous story about a fast but feckless rabbit and his foot race with a reliable but lumbering turtle. The point Aesop was making is easy enough for most of us to understand, but we remember it mostly because of the improbable visual image of a turtle racing a rabbit and winning.

When the authors of the Book of Genesis wanted to address the concept of evil in the world they told a story about Noah and his ark. The concept of God's dissatisfaction with man's evil ways on earth is hardly new, yet for most people the tale of animals marching two by two up the gangplank to be saved from rising floodwaters is a lot more memorable than any sermon. The objective is always the same, to keep the audience listening and paying attention. If telling a memorable story is good enough for the bible, it is probably good enough for the rest of us.

5 /

Taking the Stage

Reaching People One at a Time

Great communicators do not become great communicators overnight. Great speeches and presentations don't happen by accident. Preparing the right material in the right way is important, and so is intensive practice. There are a few very simple physical skills that can make all the difference in how a live audience reacts to you and what you have to say. Most of us are perfectly comfortable talking with one or two other people face to face. We do it every day and never think anything about it. But when the group gets larger most people start to get nervous. Individuals are familiar. Big groups are scary. But if you stop to think about it, any group of people, no matter how large or formidable, is actually made up of individuals. You don't have to reach the entire audience all at once, and you shouldn't try. Concentrate instead on reaching as many individuals in that audience as possible, one at a time. The best way to do that is through their eyes.

Eye Contact

The eyes are said to be the windows to the soul, and for a presenter, the eyes are the first and most powerful point of contact with the audience. Your eyes can convey your passion, enthusiasm, and honesty. The audience's eyes are always unconsciously on the prowl for fresh visual stimulation. Keeping the eyes of the audience from straying away from you is never easy, but it pays big dividends in attention and impact. So let the audience see your eyes, and practice holding the attention of individual audience members through theirs.

Here's how to do it. When you stand up to speak to a group, never just start talking. Keep your mouth closed until you have reached out silently with your eyes to an individual member of the audience. It doesn't matter who, as long as they can see you and you can see them. Lock onto that person's eyes. Look at them. Make sure they are looking at you. Someone who is not looking at you may be listening to what you say, but without strong, sustained, and direct eye contact you probably aren't reaching them as deeply or as effectively as you would like. Start talking only when you have made firm contact with the other person through their eyes. Talk directly to that person. Ignore everyone else in the room. Concentrate on that single individual until you have delivered a complete thought and you are reasonably sure they have taken it in. Only then allow yourself to break away to another individual and do the same thing all over again. Lock onto their eyes. Make sure they are paying attention. And then, and only then, allow yourself to start talking.

A complete thought may be a single sentence or several. It may be only a few words. The key is to maintain eye contact while you are talking directly to the selected individual for at least as long as it takes for the process to begin feeling uncomfortable. That's usually just about the right length of time. And never allow yourself to shift your gaze on and off the individual to whom you are speaking. This only makes the process more challenging by forcing both of you to constantly focus and refocus your attention.

In a small group you can easily make this kind of meaningful eye contact with every individual in the room, and you should. This is impossible in larger groups. But even if you manage to make sustained eye contact with only a small percentage of those in the room, it nevertheless will convey a powerful impression of personal engagement with the entire audience. This only works, however, if you are able to resist the temptation to sweep your eyes around the room in a futile effort to see and connect with everyone at once. Sweeping the room with your eyes will only overload your brain with way too much visual information, making it impossible for you to process any of it effectively. This, in turn, will just make you more nervous and less able to connect comfortably with your audience. Unless the audience is paying close attention to you with their eyes, it is unlikely that they will be absorbing very much with their ears.

Never roll your eyes. It makes you look nervous, shifty, and bored. Never look at your watch. You may only be trying to maintain your pace, but your audience will read this as a sign that you can't wait until your speaking ordeal is over. A better way to keep in touch with the time is to put your watch or a small, quiet clock on the lectern right next to your notes. Remember what happened to the first President Bush in 1992 during a televised debate with challenger Bill Clinton. The president was caught on camera looking at his watch. This perfectly ordinary and probably unconscious gesture sent the unhelpful message that the president was bored with the debate. Most voters like their politicians to be more attentive and engaged than that. The same is true for any audience you are likely to face.

Visual Aids

When it comes to getting a message across, what your audience sees has far more impact than anything they hear. As much as 90 percent of the information stored in the brain is visual. Visual aids, such as slides, paper flip charts, and physical props, can add life to almost any presentation. But visual aids should be just that, *aids* and nothing more. The power of a presentation can never depend entirely on fancy visual aids. Visuals can help you inform and persuade your audience, but by themselves, even the very best visuals are a poor substitute for an effective message and a compelling personal presence. Visual aids should never be allowed to become the center of attention. They should never be allowed to compete with you for the audience's attention. They should only be used to help you make your point. The most effective presenters use as few visuals as possible, and they always try to keep them simple. For a presentation to work *you* always have to be the news in the room. You have to be the center of attention. That's a tough assignment if you are forced to compete with a flashy slide show. Before you know it, you could well end up as nothing more than the invisible and anonymous narrator pushed into the shadows by your own slides. The audience came to see and hear you, a live human being. They didn't come to be trapped in a dark room watching a slide show. These days they can do that more conveniently at a virtual meeting Web site. No matter how sophisticated the graphic technology, slides and other visual aids are there for one purpose and one purpose only: to support you and what you have to say.

We once worked with a very charismatic CEO who had a remarkable gift for quietly inspiring his troops. He wasn't flashy. He wasn't loud or bombastic. He wasn't even a great orator in the traditional sense. He could hold an audience's attention and make a point as well as anyone, but his company had a long tradition of using very fancy graphic presentations at all its meetings. Despite our recommendation that he dump the graphics and go it alone, even the CEO couldn't fight the corporate culture and, as a result, he often found himself competing with his own slides whenever he made a presentation. We were able to make some impact, however, by getting the communications department to limit the number and complexity of the slides he used to support his presentations and by giving the CEO some tips on how to pull the audience away from the slide show and back to the speaker.

For example, when using projected slides, always try to make sure the entire audience can clearly see you, as well as the slides. Keep the room lights as bright as possible without washing out the image on the screen. If you doubt the importance of keeping the lights on during a presentation, just remember what parents often do to get a cranky baby to fall asleep. They turn the lights down low and read the child a story until he nods off. You, on the other hand, should be trying to keep your audience wide awake and listening carefully to what you have to say. The last thing you want to do is dim the lights and put the audience to sleep with a soothing slide show narration. We've all seen it happen.

Words and Pictures

When using slides or other graphics, keep them as simple as possible. Try to follow the "four-by-four rule." Four lines with no more than four words on each line. Ideally, a single slide should contain only as much information as a driver traveling at forty miles an hour can read and absorb from a roadside billboard. So never try to cram too much material onto any one slide. Just divide it up among several. When putting together your slides or charts, never use words if pictures will do the job as well. Use simple drawings and graphics whenever possible to help hold down the number of words on each slide and increase the impact of the overall presentation. Make sure your visuals are simple, colorful, and big enough for everyone in the audience to see clearly. More complicated material should be eliminated from the slides you project during your presentation and saved for distribution as handouts after you have finished speaking. Never distribute copies of your presentation before you are finished. You will not only have to compete with the slides being projected on the screen, but you will also have to work that much harder to hold the attention of those who can't resist reading ahead in the written version. While you are delivering your presentation, you want to eliminate as many distractions as possible and do everything you possibly can to focus the audience's attention on you. And always take a paper copy of your slides to the lectern with you. Even if the technology fails you completely, and it often does, you will still be able to keep going with your talk as if nothing out of the ordinary had ever ever happened.

What Works and Why

Not all visuals are created equal. Just because a particular visual looks nice on the screen doesn't necessarily mean that it will help you make your point. For example, complex systems can often be reduced to simple diagrams that anyone can understand at a glance. This map of the Washington, D.C., subway system is a typical example of a schematic visual that packs a lot of different kinds of information into a single two-dimensional diagram.

A simple bar graph is often the best way to illustrate comparisons between similar data points.

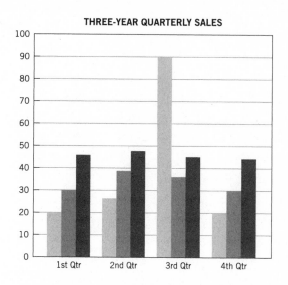

A line chart is a good way to illustrate a trend over time.

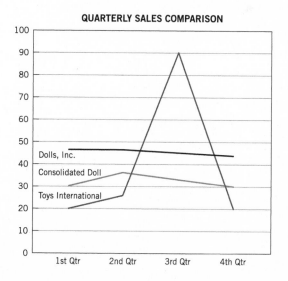

If you want to show the audience how something is divided, a pie chart is usually the best way to do it.

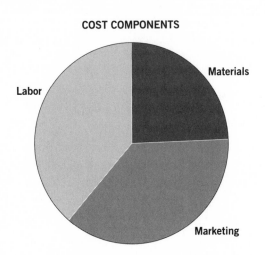

Simplicity and clarity are always the most important considerations when selecting illustrations and visual aids. Your visual aids should be colorful and interesting, of course, but if they are too detailed or complicated they may actually make it harder for you to make your point to the audience.

Clearing the Visual

One very effective technique you can use to draw the audience's attention away from the visuals and back to you during a presentation is called *clearing.* This simply means telling the audience what they are seeing on each slide or flip chart page as soon as it appears and before you start going into any detail about the material the graphic is intended to illustrate. The objective is to immediately drain the visual of any mystery, so that the audience won't still be trying to figure it out when they should be paying attention to you. For example, let's say your slide includes a complicated graph comparing annual sales figures for several divisions of the company over the past five years. As soon as the slide appears on the screen you should say something to the audience like:

> This chart shows how our sales have been doing over the past five years. You can see that we started strong but then lost ground until last year. Now, let me explain what happened in more detail.

If the slide is a list of bullet points summarizing the key challenges your department will be facing in the coming fiscal year, you could say something like:

> This slide outlines our four biggest challenges for the next year: sales growth, cost control, recruiting, and new competition. Now let's look at each in more detail.

No matter how complicated the visual may be, the audience will now have a clear idea of what it is supposed to represent in general, and they won't be distracted by reading over each bullet and trying to figure out what it means. They will have the key message.

These very simple summaries of the material on each slide will "clear" the content and allow the audience to return comfortably to you for a detailed explanation of how the material relates to the larger strategic point you want to make. You are now free to break away from the slide in order to rearrange the order of the items and perhaps even ignore some altogether. Failing to clear a slide forces the audience to keep reading and decoding all the material as it appears on the screen, while you try to recapture their attention so you can deliver your message. Unfortunately, the visual usually wins the contest. You and your message are pushed into the background.

Remember, however, that properly clearing a slide is entirely different from simply reading it aloud to the audience. Like Mrs. Thatcher, most people can do that much faster for themselves. And, if you let them, that is exactly what they will do. Above all, never expect the visuals to do your work for you. Even the slickest visual aids won't really be effective unless you are able to supplement them with your own physical energy, presence, and passion. Similarly, just because you are using fancy slides doesn't mean you can forget about effective eye contact and a powerful physical presentation. Using strong eye contact to make a personal connection with as many members of the audience as possible is even more important when you are presenting alongside a potentially distracting slide show.

Touch, Turn, Talk

A good way to remind yourself to put this principle into practice during a presentation is to remember the "touch, turn, talk rule." It works like this: As soon as a new slide or flip chart page appears, immediately relate to it physically. This is easy if you are using a paper flip chart or working in front of a small group. You can just reach over and touch the chart or the screen. It is a bit more complicated, but far from impossible, in a large room with a big screen. In that situation you simply gesture in the direction of the screen in order to create a physical connection for the audience between you and the visual. Always use your hand, never a pointer, especially a laser pointer. These clever little gadgets are lots of fun to play with, but that little red light bouncing all over a big screen can't help but distract attention from you and the material on the slide.

After establishing a clear physical connection with the visual, turn to face the audience and establish solid eye contact with a single individual before opening your mouth to speak. Remembering to touch, turn, and then talk will help keep you from inadvertently delivering your message to the slide or flip chart while your back is to the audience. It will help you avoid the temptation to read the slide out loud along with your audience. If you are creating a visual as you go (by writing on a flip chart, for example) always write first, then turn, and then speak. Never try to talk while you are writing or drawing on the chart. The same goes for the flashy visual effects that are now such a popular feature of computerized slide presentations. Treat the effect as if you were physically drawing it on the slide. Make sure it is completed and you are connecting with a specific individual in the audience before you resume speaking. Otherwise, whatever you say will be forced to compete with the action on the screen, making it very difficult for the audience to concentrate on you and what you have to say.

When presenting to a group, always try to stand to the *right* of the flip chart easel or screen, positioning the visuals on your left. The audience will be reading whatever text is on the visual from left to right. After they have read each line their eyes and attention will return naturally to the left edge of the visual, where you are standing. Try to avoid moving too far away from the easel or screen as you present. Moving away from your visuals just makes it harder to hold the audience's attention. It forces their eyes constantly to choose between you and the visual. Again, in far too many cases the flashy visual will win the contest and you will find yourself separated from the audience's field of vision and their attention.

If you are tempted to doubt how difficult it is to compete with an interesting visual, just think about what happened the last time you entered a crowded room, a bar for example, where a television set was turned on. Even with the sound cut off completely, every eye in the room is drawn constantly to that flickering screen. If only because the image is constantly changing, whatever is happening up there on that little screen will probably be the latest news in the room. No matter how exciting you are and no matter how important your message may be, trying to hold an audience's attention against that kind of competition is just about impossible. When making a presentation with flip charts or slides it is always better to bring the visuals as close as possible, so that all eyes in the room can remain comfortably focused on you and so that you can more naturally relate to your visuals.

When using a paper flip chart, always leave a blank page between illustrated sheets. Otherwise, the printing may show through the pages and distract the audience's attention. Before you begin speaking, bend the lower left corner of each page of a flip chart in order to keep the individual pages from sticking together. This makes it a lot easier to turn the pages smoothly as you move through your presentation. Always leave a few blank pages before your first chart so that the audience won't be distracted while you are trying to get their attention as you begin your presentation. When using projected slides, always put a title slide or other placeholder at the beginning so that the audience is not distracted by your first substantive slide before you begin to present. Similarly, inserting a simple holding slide at places in the presentation where you want to pause and bring the audience back to you will help you regain their attention. If there is nothing interesting to look at on the screen, the audience will have no choice but to look to you for new information and visual stimulation. Remember, your first priority is always to make the audience pay attention to you, not your visual aids.

Body Language

A Marine Corps general once said that "attitudes are more important than facts." What he meant was that if you really believe in your heart you can take that hill, you probably will, even if you and your buddies are badly outnumbered by the defenders. The same goes for effective communication. In order to get your message across to the audience you have to project a powerful positive attitude, not just with your words, but with your entire body. You have to personify your message, both vocally and visually. You have to clearly demonstrate your personal passion for the point you want to make.

Your overall presence, how you present yourself physically to the audience, and how the audience ultimately perceives and judges you, is a combination of a lot of little things that add up to an indelible first impression, one that should always be as powerful and positive as possible. In fact, overall audience reaction to a speech or presentation is usually more than 50 percent visual (how you look), less than 40 percent vocal (how you sound), and barely 10 percent verbal (what you actually say). If your physical presence and body language are not working for you, they are working against you, distracting the audience and constantly undermining your message. Body language can make or break a presentation, so never leave it to chance. The harsh truth is that when it comes to the audience's ultimate perception and reaction, *how* you say something is often far more important than *what* you actually say. How you present yourself visually and physically is a critical part of the total communications package.

With this in mind, get in the habit of letting your entire body help you communicate. Gesture not just with your hands but with your face and your eyes as well. This is especially important in a big room or when your presentation is being televised. The camera will probably zoom in close from time to time, so make sure it has something interesting to see. Always be ready for your big close-up. Volumes have been written on the subject, but when all is said and done, the very best way to put body language to work is to just let yourself be yourself. Let yourself go. Be energetic. Don't hold back. Don't expect your voice alone to convey the full power of your message. Use your entire body to communicate. Release your pent-up nervous energy productively. Trying to control your nervous energy by holding it back is a terrible waste of an enormously valuable communications asset. If you don't let your nervous energy come out naturally, you will just become more nervous and distracted. If you do let it out, your entire presentation will benefit.

Gestures

For some of us, physical gestures come naturally; for others, they just don't. When it comes to gestures, you should only do what feels right for you. If you are just not comfortable "speaking with your hands," never try to force it. You will only look mechanical and overrehearsed. But be aware that your natural gestures, whatever they may be, will always help you connect with the audience and help them remember what you have to say. Getting your entire body involved in your presentation not only helps you to explain your key points, it shows the audience you are involved and passionate about what you are saying.

For example, you can use your hands and fingers to enumerate individual points. You can use your hands to demonstrate the shape and size of an object, or even an abstract concept. You can use your hands and fingers to indicate direction, up, down, right, left. You can use your hands to make comparisons—"this big, this small." Whatever point you are trying to make, always try to be as physically descriptive as possible. Release as much energy as you can during your presentation by physically supporting the words you speak. And remember, when it comes to gestures, the size of the room matters. The bigger the room, the bigger the gesture required to get the message across to the entire audience. Make sure that even someone way back in the last row of the auditorium can clearly see and understand whatever gestures you use. Even if bold gestures are not your natural style, make sure that your arms, hands, and the rest of your body are always comfortably available to illustrate your points and support your words. When the opportunity presents itself, you want to be ready to paint vivid pictures in the air, whether or not you are also using more technologically advanced visual aids. Your own movements and gestures will be far more effective at reaching the audience than even the fanciest graphics, props, and slide shows. Nobody has ever created a flip chart or slide show that can come close to competing with the human body as a visual communication tool.

We were reminded of this several years ago when we were asked to help a CEO prepare for a very important presentation to his global sales force. The CEO came to our coaching session armed with the latest version of his slide show. But it was clear almost immediately that the slides he planned to use were all wrong. They simply wouldn't work with the talk he really wanted to give, and he knew it. But the coaching session was underway. There was no time to create a new slide show on the fly.

Rather than fold our tent and come back another day, we asked our client to put his slides aside and deliver his presentation standing in front of a blank wall, illustrating his key points by painting pictures in the air with his hands. As you might imagine, the CEO was a bit skeptical at first. But he was a good sport and went along with our unusual request. Later, when he looked at the videotape of his suddenly low-tech sales presentation he was amazed at how truly powerful it was. He had learned firsthand how effective an enthusiastic human being can be at illustrating an inspiring presentation with no mechanical assistance whatsoever—much more effective in most cases than even the slickest slide show. Our client learned a very important lesson that day. His passion, personal presence, infectious enthusiasm, and emotional connection with the audience were far more important to the people he needed to reach than any slide show his graphics department could possibly create.

Posture

Good posture makes you appear confident and in charge. The very best posture for delivering a powerful presentation is to stand up straight with your shoulders back. Place your feet squarely below your shoulders so energy can flow up to your torso and hands. Standing up when you speak improves airflow through your body. Standing helps increase your natural energy level. Standing makes you appear more in command. Never allow yourself to inadvertently contain your natural energy. Never put your hands in your pockets or lock them in front of your body or behind your back. Never fold your arms. It looks defensive and it puts an unnecessary barrier between you and the audience. Hold your ground. Don't pace or shift your feet. Pacing the stage may seem dramatic, but it tends to dissipate your natural energy unproductively and makes it harder for the audience to concentrate on what you are saying. Never try to walk and talk at the same time. It just distracts the audience. Be careful never to speak unless you are in control of your territory and are making strong, sustainable eye contact with an individual in the audience.

If you use a lectern, it should serve as a visual center of gravity, never a barrier between you and your audience. Never lean on the lectern. It is only there to hold your notes, not your body. The energy you waste clinging to the lectern, or trying to hide behind it, should be used instead to support your message with strong physical gestures. If you are sitting down for a panel discussion, position your rear end into the back of the chair. This pushes your upper body forward and makes you appear more engaged and interested while still leaving your hands free to gesture.

Get familiar with the environment in which you will be speaking well before you begin. Make it work for you not against you. Try to eliminate last-minute surprises by carefully working out ahead of time what microphones and other audiovisual equipment you will be using, where you will be located on the stage, how you will be introduced, and by whom. Give the person who will be introducing you a short written introduction. Don't depend on them to ad lib an introduction from your biography or resume. They might read the whole thing and bore the audience to death. Know ahead of time how questions and answers will be handled and where you are supposed to go when it is time to leave the stage.

Using a Prompter

Simple, reliable, and relatively inexpensive technology has in recent years made electronic prompting devices available to almost anyone speaking before a large group. Prompters are no longer exclusively for politicians, news anchors, and expensive television production studios. You can use them, too, but to do so effectively you need to keep in mind exactly what even the most sophisticated prompters can and cannot do.

Modern prompters are mostly of three types. The most common are the familiar glass plates located on stands at the speaker's eye level a few feet away from the lectern. You see them every year when the president goes before Congress to deliver his State of the Union address. A less common variation uses one or more large television monitors placed further away from the speaker, often on the floor in front of the lectern or at the back of the room. In a television studio, the prompter text will usually be displayed right in front of the camera lens, allowing the reader to look directly into the camera while reading. In all three configurations the text is displayed in letters large enough for the speaker to read easily as the words roll by.

The key to using a prompter effectively is to remember that it is only that, a prompter. Even if they cannot see the prompting equipment, modern audiences are far too sophisticated to believe that anyone, even their favorite news anchor, has really memorized all that copy, word for word. So don't pretend. Avoid focusing so completely on the text as it magically scrolls before your eyes, that you lose your critical eye contact with the audience and fall into that faraway, disconnected look we call "prompter stare." The prompter can be a very comforting security blanket, but it can also be a dangerous crutch. The prompter makes it perfectly possible, and very tempting, to just read the verbatim text as it rolls before your eyes, but it is far more effective to use the prompter much the same way you would use notes on a lectern. Especially when using a prompter, you must remember never to open your mouth to speak until you have made firm eye contact and completely engaged the attention of a specific individual in the audience.

Another trick to using a prompter naturally is to force yourself to look down at your written text or notes occasionally, both to keep your place and to break the visual monotony. A good opportunity to do this is when you are quoting something. Television anchors make their living reading prompters. The next time you tune in a television newscast, watch carefully how the anchor looks down whenever he starts to quote something the audience subconsciously expects should be read from text or notes. Reading a quote off the prompter, or failing to glance down at your copy now and then, will make the audience uncomfortable, if only subconsciously. They know perfectly well that you are using a prompter, and if you never look down at your notes, they will sense that something isn't quite right, even if they can't pin down exactly what it is.

Electronic prompters are not automatic. They come with a human operator whose job is to load your copy into the computer that feeds the screen, format the copy for easy reading in the large prompter font, and then roll the text across the screen as you read it. To make all this work smoothly, you must give the prompter operator a copy of your speech text file on a computer disk, CD, or flash drive, far enough in advance of your speech to allow time to do the loading and formatting. Even after the operator has loaded your text into his computer, don't expect to just show up at the last minute and read your speech from the prompter. Allow enough time for at least one complete run-through with the prompter operator before you go on for real. This allows the operator to get comfortable with your pace and to make sure that the font and spacing of the text on the prompter screen are completely comfortable for you.

You can ask the operator to increase or decrease the font size to suit your own eyes. Larger type is easier to read, especially at a long distance. But smaller type allows more copy to appear on the screen at once, making it easier to keep your place in the text. As you speak, the prompter operator will follow your delivery, slowing down and speeding up as you read. Since only a few lines of text will appear on the screen at once, the operator needs to know where on the screen to position the line you are currently reading. This line will be marked by a red or white arrow usually appearing at the left side of the prompter screen as you see it. Most people like to position the line they are reading in the middle or near the top of the screen. Since the copy rolls up from the bottom, this allows you to get a good look at what's coming before you read it. But you can ask the operator to position the arrow anywhere on the screen that feels the most comfortable for you. During your run-through, you might want to try it several different ways until you find what works best. The easiest way to indicate a pause on a prompter is simply to leave a big blank space. The clearest way to indicate emphasis is with boldface type. During your run-through the prompter operator can easily make these adjustments, as well any last-minute changes in wording, right on his computer. Don't hesitate to ask.

Reading from a Text

While it is always better to work from notes alone, there will be times when you have no choice but to read from a prepared text without the aid of a prompter. This is never easy, even for speakers with a great deal of experience. It's tough to read from a printed page while maintaining eye contact with the people in the audience. But there is a very effective technique, called *dip and grab,* that with a bit of practice will help you stick to the written text and still maintain that all-important eye contact and connection with your audience.

As you practice reading your speech, break the text into phrases short enough for you to read and remember at one glance. For most of us, this is about half a line or perhaps a single short sentence or phrase. Practice looking down at your printed text just long enough to grab the phrase and remember it. Then look up, make eye contact with an individual in the audience, and deliver just that phrase. Then look down again and grab the next phrase. Look up and deliver it. As always, the key is to establish and maintain eye contact whenever you are talking. Even when reading a text word for word, you should never open your mouth until you have made sustainable eye contact with an individual in the audience. Dipping down to the text in order to grab a phrase before looking up to deliver it allows you to do what might otherwise have seemed physically impossible.

All the pausing that this technique requires might feel unnatural at first, but the audience won't mind the pauses, as long as each is followed by something worth hearing. Droning on and on through your written text is exactly the wrong way to hold the audience's attention. If all you do is read to them from a prepared text—never looking up and never making eye contact—the audience will soon stop paying attention, no matter how eloquent your words may be. If you don't look at them, why should they feel any obligation to look at you? If they aren't looking at you, they will soon stop listening to you as well. As we've seen, unless you continue to connect with individual members of the audience by establishing and maintaining sustainable eye contact, their attention will quickly stray to whatever else seems new or interesting in the room. Disciplining yourself never to speak unless you are connecting with a real person, even when you are shackled to a written text, will help keep the audience's attention focused where it belongs: on you and the point you want to make.

Facial Expressions

You always want your facial expressions to support the points you are making. There are a few fairly simple but important things to remember about facial expressions. For example, even when you are not showing a full smile, try not to frown. Frowning sets up a subconscious barrier between you and your audience, diluting the impact of the eye contact you are working so hard to maintain. Lift your eyebrows slightly to open your face. It is a lot easier to connect with the audience if as many people in the room as possible can clearly see your eyes.

Facial expressions are even more important if your presentation is being televised. Television tends to magnify facial features, including lines and shadows, and pull everything down. In a television close-up, an unconscious look of minor concern may appear as extreme anger. As with any gesture, the best way to monitor and adjust your facial expressions is to practice your presentation repeatedly in front of a mirror or on videotape. When practicing a speech or presentation, always try to see yourself as others see you.

Tone of Voice

When you are delivering a speech or presentation, think of your voice as a musical instrument. Musicians often point out that music is really what happens between the notes. The artistic impact of a musical performance depends to a significant degree on modulation, the contrast between loud and soft, sound and silence. Think back to the worst speeches and presentations you have ever had to endure. They probably were delivered in something resembling a dull monotone. No highs. No lows. No pauses. Nobody sets out deliberately to sound dull, but it can happen before you know it. Great speakers go out of their way to breathe life into their delivery by carefully varying their volume, tone, and rhythm. Deliberate changes in volume and tone will make your voice more expressive and help you convey subtleties you couldn't possibly express with words alone. Your voice and delivery should be carefully styled to convey confidence and authority. Think about some of the great orators of our time: Winston Churchill, Franklin Roosevelt, John Kennedy, and Martin Luther King Jr. They all shaped their delivery as carefully as they crafted their messages. So can you.

Break away from the bondage of a dull text. Consider every presentation, no matter how large the audience happens to be, as a personal conversation with each and every individual in the room. Allow your voice to convey energy and passion. Use your physical delivery, as well as your words, to paint memorable pictures in every listener's mind.

Power of the Pause

For some reason, many people have the feeling that if they ever stop talking, the audience will automatically stop listening. In fact, just the opposite is true. If you suddenly lower your voice, or stop talking altogether, it will immediately attract your audience's attention. It makes you, for a moment at least, the latest news in the room. Pausing before making a major point alerts the audience that something important is coming up. Pausing after you make a point lets the audience absorb what you just said before you move on to something new. Strategic pauses give the audience time to reflect on what you have said. Pauses buy you time to think, so you will be less tempted to use all those *ers, ahs,* and *you knows* that will make you sound unsure and unprepared.

For your voice to be effective, you have to be heard, especially in a large room. But shouting is the wrong way to do it. Talking loudly can often convey an image of aggression and desperation. At the same time, genuine passion is always positive, and natural enthusiasm is infectious. There is no harm in showing the audience every ounce of the passion you have for your message. The "cool" approach may seem stylish and safe, but it won't get the job done if your goal is to reach the audience at an emotional level. If it's clear to them that you care, your audience will be more inclined to care as well.

Script Marking

It is often helpful to mark your text or notes with simple visual cues that will help you incorporate gestures and vocal variety in your delivery.

For example, use arrows to indicate up or down pitch. ↑ ↓

Use a single slash to indicate a pause. /

Use a double slash to indicate a complete stop or a very long pause. //

<u>Underline</u> words you want to emphasize.

Nobody alive today can remember what Abraham Lincoln sounded like when he delivered the Gettysburg Address. But here is how he might have marked the opening lines of his text for delivery:

↑ Four score and seven years ago / our forefathers brought forth upon this continent a <u>new</u> nation / conceived in liberty / and dedicated to the proposition that <u>all</u> men are created equal //

↓ Now / we are engaged in a great civil war / testing whether <u>that</u> nation / or <u>any</u> nation / so conceived and so dedicated / can long endure.

Try reading the passage out loud for yourself, first as you see it in the textbooks and then from the marked script. And remember, conventional punctuation marks are intended for a text being read silently on a printed page. When you deliver a speech or presentation to a live audience they never see the text. So you have to create all the necessary punctuation with your voice. When speaking to an audience your goal is to be as naturally conversational as possible. Sentence fragments are fine. A flat, mechanical delivery is not. Again, in addition to one or more intensive table reads, you should take the time to practice your delivery as often as possible in front of a mirror or a video camera. If possible, practice in front of friends or coworkers and ask for their feedback. See how well you can hold their attention by modulating your voice, releasing your natural energy, and working to establish and maintain individual eye contact.

Appearance

You always want the audience to concentrate on what you are saying rather than what you are wearing. Nothing you wear should ever be allowed to distract from what you have to say. But beyond that, feel free to wear whatever feels natural and comfortable for you. For men, this is often a basic navy blue suit or blazer, a light-to-medium-blue shirt, and a red or other brightly colored necktie. For women, a tailored jacket, knee-length skirt, bright hues of navy blue, purple, deep pink, green, or turquoise, and low-heeled pumps. If the room is large and brightly lit, consider using makeup similar to what would be appropriate for an on-camera television interview. These days, whether to wear a tie is often an issue. There is no fixed definition of "business casual," but most people assume it means not wearing a tie or, for women, wearing pants instead of a skirt. If you are familiar with the environment in which you will be speaking and the audience you will be facing, the decision about how to dress probably will be easy. But if you aren't sure how others will be dressed or how they will expect you to look, it pays to be cautious. For men, if everyone else is dressed casually you can always take your tie off, but if you are the only person who shows up without a tie, it may be hard to find one at the last minute. For women, even these days, a skirt or dress is usually more universally appropriate, and therefore a safer choice than pants.

Taking Questions

Some speakers consider the question-and-answer period that often follows a formal presentation to be either a pointless throwaway or an outright annoyance. But, if you handle it properly, the question-and-answer session can be the single most important part of your performance. Questions and answers give the audience a chance to direct the discussion to what they consider most important. Questions and answers give you an opportunity to reinforce your key messages at a time when the audience is likely to be paying especially close attention. If the format of your presentation allows, you should always try to leave as much time as possible for questions and answers and try to make the most of the opportunity. But first you have to get the ball rolling.

The best way to encourage questions from the audience is simply to raise your hand. This alerts everyone that something new is about to happen, and it shows them exactly how they can participate. All they have to do is raise their hand, just as you are doing. If you merely stand there and ask if anyone has a question, most people in the audience will probably hesitate to get involved. But if you show them very clearly, and very physically, how they can join the discussion, a lot more will feel comfortable doing so. Assuming you see more than one hand go up, it is now your turn to choose your questioner. Most of us are naturally inclined to point to the person we have chosen. But pointing your finger sends a very negative message. It tends to make the person being pointed at feel uncomfortable. It's like putting them on the spot. An open hand, palm up, is far less threatening and far more likely to convey a positive feeling to your audience. When selecting a questioner don't worry about first come, first served. You control who gets to ask questions. If there is someone in the audience who you know from previous experience will be antagonistic or likely to pull the discussion off track, you are under no obligation to call on them, even though they may have put their hand in the air before anyone else.

As each question is being asked, maintain strong eye contact with the questioner. Listen carefully. But when the person asking the question is finished, immediately break off eye contact and turn to someone else in the audience. Begin your answer only after you have established eye contact with that other person. It may seem more logical and natural to address your answer to the person who asked the question, but this can easily leave the rest of the audience feeling ignored. Unless the question happens to concern something they also care about, it gives others in the audience a subconscious excuse to stop paying attention. The purpose of the question-and-answer session is to hold the attention of the entire audience, not engage in a dialogue with any one person.

Shifting to another member of the audience also gives you a valuable opportunity to rephrase the question that has been asked. Just as you are under no obligation to answer questions on a first come, first served basis, you should feel perfectly free to assert your control over the process by reframing questions on your own terms before answering them. Rephrasing in this way allows you to turn a negative question into one you can address positively. It allows you to make any question, no matter how specific to the individual questioner, relevant to the entire audience. Rephrasing makes it easier for you to bridge from your response to the point you want to make. Perhaps most important, breaking away from the original questioner and taking time to rephrase will give you a few extra seconds to think about just how you want to answer. Answering questions gives you a further opportunity to deliver your message. Rephrasing and bridging allows you to turn any question into an opportunity to reinforce your key message and make your point with the audience.

Keep your answers brief. Use no more than a few seconds to address the specific question. Take a few more seconds to bridge, and then use the rest of the time available to deliver your message. If you ignore the question entirely and just launch into your key message, your credibility will suffer and you will lose the audience's attention. On the other hand, if you take too long to get to the point, the audience might lose focus and miss it entirely. Watch the audience carefully. If it starts to become more difficult to maintain eye contact, you are probably going on too long. Wrap up your answer and take another question.

One thing you can never control, of course, is the questioner's attitude. You have to be prepared for hostility. But in the face of hostile questioning, always keep your cool. Remember, you are in control. You can rephrase even the most hostile question positively and then isolate the hostile questioner by delivering your positive answer to the audience as a whole. Just to be on the safe side, after you prepare your list of the most difficult issues you think you could face, practice rephrasing and bridging to your key message until you are completely comfortable with the process. Remember never to repeat negative statements or pejorative words or phrases when rephrasing or answering tough questions.

Presentation Preparation Checklist

Run through the following checklist before taking the stage to deliver a speech or presentation:

- Eat lightly. Just enough to maintain your energy level.
- Avoid alcohol, caffeine, and carbonated beverages before speaking.
- Arrive early and check out your speaking location, including the lights, the temperature, the arrangement of the stage, the setup of the lectern, and the location of the microphone.
- Double-check the audiovisual arrangements, including projectors and computers. Make sure you are comfortable operating them.
- If you are using a prompter, make sure the operator has your text in plenty of time to load it into his computer.

- Do at least one complete run-through with the prompter operator to make sure the text is right and you are comfortable with the setup.
- Bring an extra hard copy of your notes or text, just in case the prompter equipment fails.
- If you are using a PowerPoint or other slide presentation, bring an extra copy on disc, CD, or flash drive and have a hard copy of your slides with you at the lectern, just in case the projector fails.
- Run through your slides on the screen where they will be projected, just to make sure they look the way you expect.
- Meet the person who will introduce you and give them your own brief introduction on a single sheet of paper or a 3-by-5 card.
- Have a glass of water (room temperature, no ice) available at the lectern or where you will be seated during your presentation.
- Know the main point you want to make, the message you want to deliver, and be prepared to deliver it with every ounce of physical energy and passion you can muster.
- Know exactly where you are supposed to go when you have finished speaking.

As you begin speaking, keep the following in mind:

- Establish firm eye contact with an individual in the audience before you open your mouth to speak.
- Be relaxed and natural, but release as much energy as you can by being visual and physically descriptive. Use your entire body to support the words you are speaking.

- Never put your hands in your pockets or fold them in front or behind your body or across your chest.
- Stand with your feet placed squarely below your shoulders. Don't pace or shift your feet.
- *Touch* each visual that you use as soon as you show it, then *turn* to an individual in the audience and establish firm eye contact before you *talk*.
- Stay as close as possible to the easel or screen. Never use a pointer.
- Raise your hand to signal when you are ready to receive questions.
- Use an open hand to acknowledge a question.
- Look at the questioner and listen carefully. Maintain eye contact.
- Before answering, break visually from the questioner and repeat or rephrase the question, being careful never to repeat negative statements or pejorative words or phrases.
- Stand back from the lectern and don't grip it.
- Never touch the microphone.

6 /

The Media Landscape

Knowing the Rules and Winning the Game

A long time ago the British press baron Lord Northcliffe made the clever observation that anything someone doesn't want published is journalism and everything else is just advertising. For better or worse, the modern media environment is a lot more complicated than that. The media are all around us all the time. We interact with them every day, often without even being consciously aware of it. Whether we like to admit it or not, the media are also a powerful reflection of both the best and the worst aspects of our own basic human nature. Today's media landscape is changing so rapidly that it is very difficult for anyone to navigate—even professional communicators who work in and with the media every day. But a clear understanding of how the media operate is absolutely essential to effective strategic communication. You need to understand and appreciate how the media really work if you are to have any chance at all of working with them to reach your strategic objectives. There are a number of practical tools and techniques that will help you attract media attention, prepare efficiently for media interviews, connect with the audience, focus your message for maximum impact, handle hostile questioning, keep control of an interview, and reach your strategic objectives by helping the media reach theirs.

Lots and Lots of Media

Before looking at how to handle individual media interviews, however, it is important to note that media today include newspapers, magazines, conventional broadcast outlets, as well as the Internet and all the new forms of media it has spawned, including the World Wide Web, blogs, streaming audio and video, video-sharing Web sites such as YouTube, audio and video podcasting, instant messaging, broadband audio and video delivery to cell phones, and even social networking Web sites such as MySpace. The bright lines that once clearly defined the nature of news and the way it is distributed are rapidly fading. Most of what was once considered purely print journalism is now being distributed electronically. Newspaper Web sites routinely carry audio and video as well as text and still pictures. Traditional television broadcasting has morphed into cable and satellite delivery. Cable systems and direct broadcast satellite services routinely offer hundreds of digital program channels. Terrestrial broadcast radio is being challenged by direct satellite distribution and Internet radio. Digital multicasting allows terrestrial radio stations to broadcast multiple channels in high-definition audio. And surveys show that most people now consider

---

* "Five Years Later—Media Perceptions from 2002 to 2007," Internet and Multimedia 2007 Report (Somerville, NJ: Edison Media Research, 2007), http://www.edisonresearch.com/home/archives/Q3%20Media%20Perceptions%20-%20large%20slides%20_2_.pdf.

the Internet to be more "essential" to their lives than radio.* All across the media landscape scarcity is giving way to extreme fragmentation. Big stories are being broken every day on blogs, both professional and amateur, before they are picked up by the so-called "mainstream media." Newsworthy video often appears on YouTube and other video-sharing Web sites long before it reaches television newscasts. Just ask any of the unlucky politicians who have awakened after a long day on the campaign trail to find an embarrassing video clip spreading like a virus across the Internet. Even many working journalists are no longer quite sure just what "journalism" really means in today's complicated media environment. But despite all this technological innovation and market fragmentation, and no matter how the news is defined or ultimately delivered to the audience, the fundamental rules of strategic communication still apply.

In fact, while the names may sound new and exotic, the essentials of information distribution still remain much the same. For example, blogs are really nothing more than personal (or perhaps not so personal) Web pages made available for free to anyone with Internet access. Looked at another way, today's millions of bloggers might be considered direct descendants of the pamphleteers and street corner orators of a much earlier age. Only the distribution technology is different, and it keeps changing at a faster and faster pace. Instant messaging and, texting, are really just alternate forms of e-mail. The ability to instantly and inexpensively post text, audio, and video on a Web page is really nothing new either. Just about every news organization and millions of ordinary individuals have been doing it every day for years. Embedding links to other sites have always been fundamental to the syntax of Web content. More recent innovations such as RSS are just a simple way of automatically monitoring and aggregating multiple Web feeds for convenient access. Setting up a Google news alert takes a minute or two and lets anyone with an e-mail connection instantly receive the latest news about anyone or anything that happens to interest them. Podcasting is not all that different from taping a broadcast on your VCR or downloading it to a DVR for replay at a more convenient time. Only the technology for storage and delivery has changed.

For all their similarities, however, the Web and its many off-shoots are more than just a new way to deliver old media content in a faster and more convenient fashion. The unique characteristics of the Web, at least as it has evolved so far, are interactivity, interconnectivity, and bandwidth. Unlike traditional print and electronic media, the Web gives every user the ability to request what they want and respond instantly to anything they see or read. Sending a letter to the editor and hoping it gets printed is one thing. Adding comments to a blog posting and seeing them appear instantly and generate further comment is quite another. The Web is also built on the notion that all sources of information can and should be interconnected. On the Web, what might have been a short footnote in a traditional print publication becomes an instant electronic link to a potentially infinite library of primary sources and background information. Web search tools such as Google and Yahoo! further facilitate the process by finding and organizing catalogs of links that lead instantly to related sources of information. These new aspects of online and interactive media are important also because they contradict what has long been the most fundamental element of the editorial process. Traditional print and broadcast journalism is still based on the management of scarcity, how best to make use of very limited space and time. Web editors face exactly the opposite challenge: how to manage an abundance of information and how to make sense of an infinite amount of raw material available to anyone at the click of a mouse. But regardless of how exotic the technology, both the old and the new media serve the same needs of the same audiences—the same audiences you are trying to reach with your message.

Challenges and Opportunities

This increasingly complicated media environment offers both challenges and opportunities to anyone trying to make a point to an important audience. Never before in history has so much information been so widely distributed to so many people at such great speed. Gone forever are the days when orderly "news cycles" were defined by the daily deadlines of morning newspapers and evening network news shows. Today, as soon as something newsworthy happens anywhere in the world, people expect to hear about it instantly, and see it live as it happens. Even "spy in the sky" surveillance satellite photographs, once the top-secret tool of government intelligence agencies, are now routinely used by news organizations to illustrate their stories, and anyone with an Internet connection can instantly retrieve a satellite image of any street address or a live feed from thousands of traffic surveillance cameras. Live television coverage from news helicopters has become a cliché in many markets. Big stories are often covered first by amateur eyewitnesses shooting pictures with their cell phones. Thanks to modern news-gathering and distribution technology, no corner of the planet is any longer so remote as to be invisible to the probing eyes and ears of the news media or unreachable by their insatiable audiences. Reading any of thousands of newspapers and magazines requires nothing more than a decent Internet connection. No more waiting for mail delivery or crawling through the bushes looking for a wet newspaper. Whatever the hour of the night or day, and wherever we may be in the world, none of us is very far from a live feed of the latest news in text, audio, or video format.

It used to be that a call from a national network news broadcast was the worst nightmare any corporate communications department could imagine. These days the really good stuff is more likely to show up first on YouTube long before the networks even hear about it. Consider what happened when a local television station in New York City ran video of rats scampering around a Taco Bell restaurant in Greenwich Village. Bad enough that the ugly pictures made it to the air in the country's largest market, but within hours the video had been captured by amateur bloggers and uploaded to the Web for all the world to see. What once would have been a fairly routine, if troublesome, local health inspection story was now national news, and a serious threat to the nationwide Taco Bell brand. Yum! Brands, the company that owns Taco Bell, initially tried to handle the situation as a local story. They were slow to realize how rapidly the video of their rat problem was spreading in cyberspace and how badly their corporate reputation was being damaged as a result. Within a few hours a Google search on the phrase *rats and Taco Bell* turned up more than six hundred stories from around the world. And, unlike yesterday's newspapers that quickly find their way to the bottom of a birdcage, or traditional television broadcasts that disappear instantly into the ether, anything that finds its way to the Web— and these days that's just about everything—lasts forever, mistakes and all.

Around the same time that Taco Bell was dealing with its rodent crisis, the discount airline JetBlue was trying to cope with a very different situation, but one which is every bit as serious for an airline as food safety and hygiene are for a restaurant. Thanks to a sudden ice storm over the Valentine's Day weekend, hundreds of JetBlue passengers found themselves trapped in planes stuck on the runway unable to take off or return to the gate. The unfortunate passengers waited for hours while JetBlue's shorthanded operations department tried with little success to sort things out. Both United and American faced very similar situations around the same time, but they both brushed off complaints with suggestions that passengers who had been stuck on the runway for four or five hours, or in some cases left stranded for days at small airports far from their destinations, were somehow overreacting to a relatively minor inconvenience. JetBlue took a different approach, going straight to the Web to apologize, accept responsibility, announce changes in their procedures, and promote a "passengers' bill of rights," in effect challenging their competition to follow suit. The key here was not only that JetBlue made all the right moves as far as basic crisis management was concerned (more on this later), but also that it took advantage of the powerful tools of modern online media before those same tools could be turned against it by angry customers or clever competitors.

One of the most perplexing failures to use the right tools to deal effectively with what could have been a corporate crisis of significant proportions involved that icon of modern communications technology, the ubiquitous BlackBerry. One evening, when a switch to new software didn't go as planned, large parts of the BlackBerry nationwide network suddenly went dark with no warning or explanation. One would think that a company whose entire business is built around delivering e-mail would have instantly turned to the Internet to get the word out to its millions of customers, explaining what was going on and reassuring them that the situation was being brought under control. Instead, the company didn't say anything at all until news organizations started to notice their own BlackBerrys going dead and began digging into the story. Just another example of a company that should have known better fundamentally misunderstanding the rules of the new media environment.

Welcome to the Blogosphere

Blogs and other new media outlets are rapidly evolving their own rules of the road. Those who are familiar and comfortable with old ways of doing things may not approve, but the new media are here to stay, and they present both challenges and opportunities to anyone trying to reach their rapidly growing audiences. The challenges are all too obvious. These days anything anyone does or says anywhere could easily be in range of a cell phone camera. So-called amateur video is now a staple of mainstream news broadcasts, not to mention YouTube and millions of other Web sites, all easily accessible to anyone in the world with an Internet connection. For better or worse, we now live in the era of the "citizen journalist."

Dr. Peter Rost used to work for a large global pharmaceutical company. Now he spends a lot of his time publishing a personal blog devoted to what he claims are shady practices by his former employers. *Fortune* magazine once called Rost "the drug industry's most annoying—and effective—online scourge."* Quite a compliment for a news outlet that consists of nothing more than one person, an Internet connection, and, of course, thousands of devoted readers anxious to add their two cents by sending tips

---

* John Simon, "A Big Pharma Whistleblower Blogs on Drugs," *Fortune*, June 11, 2007, http://money.cnn.com/magazines/fortune/fortune_archive/2007/06/11/100061497/index.htm?section=money_latest.

and posting comments. But not really all that surprising in today's freewheeling media environment. Blogs like Rost's are designed to encourage and enable feedback from anyone who wants to participate. Anyone with embarrassing information about a big drug company's business practices can send it to Rost with the click of a mouse, and Rost can just as quickly put it on his blog for all the world to see, along with whatever commentary he chooses to add himself. Comments from readers and links to other sites spread the information further and further through the blogosphere. It doesn't take long for the best stories to be picked up by the more widely read mainstream media. Gone forever are the days when urban legends were spread slowly by word of mouth and chain letters. Today, a disgruntled whistle-blower anywhere in the world has instant access to essentially the same potential audience as the *New York Times* online, but without the moderating influence of editors and fact-checkers, and with no assurance whatever that anything they may decide to post is accurate, balanced, or fair.

This uncomfortable state of affairs has led many organizations to treat the Web and the blogosphere as a threat, something they must defend themselves against, not something they might take advantage of in order to pursue their own communications strategy. No doubt there are times when a strong defense is called for, but any such reaction should always be handled cautiously and strategically. For example, just because a particular Web site happens to be accessible to millions on the Internet doesn't mean that anyone is actually reading it or linking to it, much less taking it seriously. Web audiences, like all media consumers, usually turn out to be a lot more intelligent and discerning than critics give them credit for. We once wrote daily posts for a client's blog that drew perhaps a half-dozen comments and cross-links in a year, even though the topics were arguably of considerable interest to a potentially large, Web-savvy audience. The very fact that there are so many millions of blogs springing up every year makes it less likely that any one of them will attract enough attention to be troublesome. Overreacting to critical blog posts only risks making a bad story worse and handing opponents more negative material to spread around the Web. For all the concern that Dr. Rost's whistle-blower Web site has generated within the pharmaceutical community, and notwithstanding the publicity he has attracted in some mainstream publications, there is little evidence so far that he is having much of an impact on the broader debate over pharmaceutical industry practices. The day may come when influential blogs begin to set the media agenda, but that day has not arrived yet. For a viral video to make the leap from YouTube to the mainstream still requires a more conventional news organization to notice it and take an interest.

Using the Web and the blogosphere proactively to promote your point of view is usually a better approach than trying to chase down every online allegation and reacting to it. There are now communications firms that specialize in generating proactive buzz on the Internet and actively engaging in conversations in the blogosphere on behalf of their clients. They are experts at evaluating the relative impact of various blogs, tracking online debates, and strategically engaging the blogosphere on its own terms and in its own unique style. For example, we once represented a coalition of trade associations concerned about a rather complicated issue that mattered a lot to its members but which was almost invisible to ordinary consumers. In an effort to make the issue matter to consumers, the coalition engaged in an aggressive program of online advocacy. In short order the Internet experts they hired not only succeeded in getting a jump on opponents in the growing online debate, but also managed to change the entire context of the conversation. Instead of the debate being dismissed as a fight between two competing corporate interests, the blogosphere began to frame it as a consumer protection battle, ordinary people being abused by a powerful monopoly, a much friendlier field for our side to fight on. And just as there are experts to whom you can turn to help communicate positively on the Internet, there are now firms whose only mission is to use the latest Internet technology to protect and repair a damaged online reputation. For example, if you discover that your competitors or your opponents in a public debate are manipulating Internet search engines like Google and Yahoo! to damage your reputation by highlighting negative information and suppressing anything positive about you or your organization, these specialized firms can help you fight back by using their own Internet expertise to make sure that positive information about you shows up first in a search.

These are not stealth campaigns. Trying to secretly game the system is usually counterproductive. The smart players make no effort to hide what they are doing. They are quite open about whom they represent online. They know all too well how easy it is for tricksters to get caught and exposed by suspicious bloggers and how damaging that can be to the client's credibility. The object of the exercise is simply to establish a voice in the debate. A well-made argument will gather support on its own merits. It may not convince everyone, especially since the other side is free to join the debate as well, but it will get your voice heard in an increasingly important forum. The key is first to track the online discussion very carefully, so you are never surprised by something that suddenly gets traction in the blogosphere, and then to participate in the debate openly and vigorously, making your point just as you would in any other medium.

What Makes News?

Whether it is delivered by new media or old, news is often defined broadly as new information of significant interest to a particular audience at a particular time. Extending that definition a bit, we could say that to be considered news, a story must be *new, true,* and *relevant.* News must be new, at least to a particular audience. History has its place, but nothing is less relevant to readers and viewers, or more annoying to reporters and editors, than yesterday's news. At the same time, however, as we all find ourselves in an environment of instant twenty-four-hour news gathering and delivery, the meaning of *new* is itself changing rapidly. Yesterday's news used to be just that, something that happened twenty-four hours ago and was then reported and analyzed in the morning paper or on a network evening newscast. We had to wait a week or more to see color pictures of even the biggest news events. A generation earlier, the only video coverage available of even the most important events was the weekly movie theater newsreel. Today, something that happened barely an hour ago, even if it attracted the immediate attention and concern of a significant number of people at the time, might already be too old for the media to bother with any longer.

It goes without saying that news must be *true.* Falsehoods, and even half truths, are quickly and properly written off by an increasingly skeptical public as self-serving spin or propaganda. Not only will an untrue message quickly be rejected by the audience, but the credibility of the person who tries to deliver it will be damaged, perhaps irretrievably. Moreover, beyond simple truth and accuracy, today's skeptical news consumers increasingly demand transparency with respect to context. Your interpretation of the facts should fit your strategic objective, of course, but it must also ring true to the audience. You may be tempted to try spinning your way into the hearts and minds of your audience, but in today's intense information environment it simply won't work. The best communicators never resort to spin. Instead, they pay close attention to how a message can be framed and delivered for maximum positive impact with a specific audience. There is a big difference. Politicians still routinely practice spin, of course. And they often get away with it, but only because the public expects so little of them in the first place. Unless you are running for office, the public is likely to hold you to a much higher standard than they will the average politician delivering his self-serving sound bites on a morning talk show. Be prepared to deliver your message forcefully and articulately, but never try to ignore a legitimate question, shade the truth, or otherwise mislead the audience. If you do, you may be incinerated by the backfire.

To be effective, the message you deliver also must be *relevant* to the audience served by the news organization doing the interview. No broadcast news organization, print publication, or Web site is designed or intended to serve everyone all the time. Despite the relatively large audience and circulation figures that some national and global news organizations still boast, there is no longer any such thing as a truly mass audience for news. The modern media landscape has been transformed into a colorful tapestry of niche outlets serving narrow audiences. Even the largest circulation daily newspaper in the country, *USA Today,* is written primarily for a very specific demographic group, businesspeople on the road. Its closest competitor in circulation, *The Wall Street Journal,* is likewise aimed squarely at a specialty business audience. The mass audience that the network evening news broadcasts once served is now barely half of what it was just a generation ago. Meanwhile, audiences for more narrowly targeted cable news outlets have exploded. And more and more major news stories are originating on Web sites and blogs, many of which are not even operated by journalists in the traditional sense of the term.

What the Media Want

Given such a broad definition of news, however, the editors and producers who actually decide which stories will be covered on any given day usually follow some rather simple guidelines when deciding what is newsworthy. For example, the more people in the audience that a particular story is likely to affect, the greater its potential news value. News about your local neighborhood is unlikely to be of much interest beyond that very small geographic area, while a story that affects millions of people across the country is much more likely to attract national media attention. The more unusual the story, the more interesting it will be to reporters and editors. It is one of the oldest clichés in the news business. A dog biting a man is no big deal, but if a man bites a dog, that's big news, simply because it doesn't happen very often.

The quicker a story reaches the public, the greater the attention it will attract. Live helicopter coverage of pointless freeway car chases in Los Angeles is guaranteed to attract huge numbers of viewers, at least for a while. Most people just can't resist the temptation to slow down and take a look as they pass an automobile accident. The great magician and escape artist Harry Houdini was once asked why so many people showed up over and over again to see him repeat essentially the same old trick, slipping out of chains and handcuffs. Houdini's answer was simple. Nobody wants to see another human being die, he explained, but we all want to be there when it happens. Modern technology allows the media to bring just about any story happening anywhere to all of us instantly, live. These days you don't even need to be near a radio or television set. If something is being shown live on the air it is almost certainly available on the Internet, accessible from the comfort of your desk or on your cell phone screen. Millions of people routinely receive e-mail alerts sent automatically to their BlackBerrys whenever big news breaks.

The more visual the story, the more likely it will be to attract television coverage. Television, after all, is all about pictures, and even the most serious television news organization will probably play up an exciting picture, regardless of its inherent news value. Indeed, for today's television news viewer the picture is often the news itself. A television news organization's ability to get that helicopter feed or satellite picture may well determine how prominently a story will appear in the broadcast, or even if it appears at all. On the other hand, stories that are difficult to visualize or complicated to illustrate, regardless of how important they may otherwise be, are far less likely to play prominently on television news broadcasts.

The strongest stories always have clearly defined *victims and villains.* Indeed, a time-tested formula for investigative reporting involves first finding a victim, then recounting their tale of woe, and then publicly exposing whoever caused them to suffer. Interestingly, when developing this kind of story the reporter or news organization usually has a number of options from which to choose when it comes to identifying the villain of the piece. If you are unlucky enough to find yourself involved in this kind of story, try not to inadvertently volunteer for the villain's role. Avoid saying or doing anything that might allow the reporter or anyone else to single you out as an easy target for blame. Try to give the news organization a good reason to look elsewhere for their villain.

We were was once called upon to advise a client considering whether to agree to an interview request from a *60 Minutes* producer preparing a story about a controversial government program that was allegedly using one of the company's products in a dangerous way. The producer wanted a lot of specific factual information, as well as an on-camera interview with someone in the company who could talk about the program and the product. For all the obvious reasons, we almost always advise our clients to take advantage of an opportunity to tell their story to the media rather than let someone else do it for them. But this case turned out to be a bit different. The more we looked into the situation the more it became obvious that our client really didn't have a very strong story to tell. They had made a lot of mistakes in handling their product, which, while not directly relevant to the story itself, could have easily come out during the course of the reporting and almost certainly would have been the subject of questions during the interview. So we advised our client to be as helpful to the *60 Minutes* producers as they possibly could when it came to providing information, but not to agree to an on-camera interview. We knew that *60 Minutes* already had the victims on tape. The damage was done, and there was nothing our client or anyone else could do to fix it. But we also knew that there were other potential villains that CBS could go after. We knew, for example, that at least one government official was actually anxious to go on-camera to defend the controversial program. We also knew that *60 Minutes* wasn't looking for a lot of villains. One would do just fine to balance the story, as long as they were willing to be interviewed. In the end, our assessment of the situation proved correct. The government official was so arrogant, so sure of himself, and so poorly prepared for the interview, that he instantly became the centerpiece of the story. The perfect villain. Our client and their product ended up as a mere footnote. The overall theme of the story could easily have been corporate irresponsibility. Instead it became government arrogance and official incompetance.

While most of our strategic communications work is with big companies and others more likely to be cast by the media as villains than victims, there are occasionally exceptions. One was particularly interesting. Our client was approached by *60 Minutes* to be interviewed for a story about the online real estate business. He was a pioneer in the online discount brokerage business, and his company was one of the first victims of an organized campaign by the traditional real estate brokers to crush potential online competitors. At first, CBS was just looking for background information. The theme of the story was still unclear, but it looked like a lot of time would be spent explaining an antitrust complaint that the Justice Department had filed against the National Association of Realtors charging that their rules were anticompetitive and stacked against online brokers and bargain-hunting home buyers. But, true to the *60 Minutes* formula, the producers were quick to pick up on our client's very appealing personal story. In this case the producers had their villain, but to complete the story they still needed a sympathetic victim. Our client looked like a very good candidate.

Once we established our client's strategic interest in the story and how we wanted him to appear to the audience, we set about positioning him to fit the role that *60 Minutes* needed him to play. That made it more likely that he would actually get on the air to make his point, rather than remain merely a behind-the-scenes source of information. Because so much conversation had already taken place between our client and the CBS producers, it was easy to predict what questions he would be asked when it came time to sit down for the on-camera interview. We carefully refined his responses and made sure that he was completely comfortable making the transition from answer to message. We coached him through videotaped practice interviews to make absolutely sure that what he wanted to say would come across as intended on the screen.

As things turned out, our client's toughest challenge was helping the surprisingly ill-prepared *60 Minutes* correspondent understand the modern real estate business. Apparently the producers had failed to brief her adequately ahead of time, assuming that she was as familiar with the subject as they had become over the course of a year of research and reporting. That may have made for some tense moments behind the scenes at CBS, but for us it was a relatively minor glitch. None of the correspondent's confusion was ever going to get on the air anyway, and our client was still able to do exactly what he came to do—deliver his strategic message and make his point so that the audience would understand and appreciate it. The rest of the segment really didn't matter that much to us, as long as our client was strategically positioned as a victim and was able to make his larger point about the inevitable evolution of the real estate business and how it would benefit both brokers and buyers.

Reporters are always looking for *winners and losers.* For example, critics often decry the "horse race" aspect of political campaign coverage, but that criticism is largely misplaced. Political reporters understand as well or better than the rest of us that "issues" are important in political campaigns. But they also know that their readers and viewers are a lot more interested in who is winning the race than they are in learning who stands where on any issue. Winners and losers are always a key element in the plot of any good story.

In the end, all news judgments are somewhat subjective and

decidedly unscientific. There are no hard-and-fast rules that govern how reporters, editors, and producers decide what's newsworthy on any given day. Indeed, two different publications may select entirely different content for their stories, even when they have access to identical information. And no two journalists will ever agree on what is the day's most important, interesting, or entertaining story. For example, when controversial religious and political leader the Rev. Jerry Falwell died suddenly on a relatively slow news day, two of the three national evening newscasts, CBS and NBC, predictably led with an obituary. But ABC decided to bury the story down deep in the broadcast, for reasons it later had difficulty explaining to critics who charged that the decision reflected what they considered the network's left-wing bias. Despite some questionable comments about Falwell from the ABC anchor, the charge of deliberate bias was almost certainly unfair. It was simply a matter of subjective news judgment. This was hardly the first or last time that a story many people would assume to be a natural lead didn't make it to the top of everyone's news agenda. Timing is also important. A story that might top the news agenda one day could end up in the back of the paper the next day, simply because there are suddenly much bigger stories to report. On a broader scale, the national news agenda, print and broadcast, can usually accommodate no more than three big stories at any one time. When a fresher story emerges, one of the others inevitably will be pushed aside, no matter how important it may have seemed as recently as yesterday. Some of us are old enough to remember when manned space flight was still a novelty that demanded live and continuous coverage. Today, even after two catastrophic mishaps, most space shuttle launches barely rate a mention in the media, unless, of course, something goes tragically wrong.

The relevance of news varies from country to country and among various types of media. If you work with the media internationally, it is important to be aware of cultural and political sensitivities. For example, stories that are of routine interest to readers in Europe or Japan may be absolutely taboo for journalists in Indonesia or Malaysia. A perfectly respectable mass-market London tabloid newspaper routinely prints pictures of bare breasted young women on its inside pages. It is hard to imagine seeing something like that in a newspaper anywhere in the Middle East or even the United States. As much as modern technology has allowed news coverage and delivery to range across national borders, the news media of every country and region are still very much a reflection of their local culture. You can never assume that a story of proven interest in one country will generate the same level of interest anywhere else. For example, radio news in many countries tends to focus on political, economic, financial, and other serious subjects, while in other countries just the opposite is true. In some countries (France is a good example) the major metropolitan newspapers concentrate on analysis and opinion rather than breaking hard news. In other countries sensational tabloids rule the roost in print and serious news is more often left to radio and television. Talk radio is now a familiar, if sometimes controversial, feature of the American media landscape, but in many other countries it is of minor importance or entirely unheard of. Countries like China, with a strong interest in controlling the news their populations are allowed to receive, routinely try to restrict public access to international satellite television transmissions and the Internet.

While the media differ from country to country around the world, international media outlets such as CNN and other global channels often cover news for audiences in many different countries and cultures at once, and there are significant aspects of the modern media environment that are common to all parts of the world. For example, attention spans are shrinking everywhere. News organizations everywhere must work harder to hold the public's attention in an increasingly competitive marketplace. It is no accident that we are seeing more graphics, fewer words, and shorter quotes in both print and broadcast news produced just about everywhere. Media everywhere are responding to the public's increasing demand for more information delivered more quickly.

How the News Media Work

When preparing for a media interview you are likely to encounter at least three general types of reporters: *general assignment,* specialty or *beat,* and *investigative.* As the name suggests, the general assignment reporter is a generalist. General assignment reporters usually don't begin with an in-depth knowledge of the stories they cover. Especially in the electronic media, the general assignment reporter's job is to gather enough information, as quickly as possible, to produce an interesting story and then move on.

The specialty or beat reporter, on the other hand, will probably come to the interview already knowing a good bit about what you do and how you do it. The beat reporter's job is to develop and maintain sources and gain some expertise about particular issues. If the reporter has been on the beat for a while he or she is likely to be familiar with you and your organization. This can work either for or against you during an interview, depending upon how you handle the situation.

An investigative reporter is probably looking for trouble. Investigative reporters must be handled carefully. Some automatically adopt an antagonistic attitude when they conduct interviews.

Others take a more laid-back approach. Some style themselves as crusaders out to save the world. Others are more reasonable and down to earth. But by definition, investigative reporting is always about digging up dirt and making things happen, usually bad things from your point of view. An investigative reporter or investigative team may spend months working on a single story, gathering data, and acquiring an understanding of the issues involved. By the time you meet for an interview the reporter will probably know a great deal about you, your organization, and the story at hand. By the time your turn comes, the reporter or producer may already have interviewed many other sources, including those on the other side of the issue. Some local television news organizations employ flamboyant investigative reporters whose stock in trade is often more showmanship than substance. They may or may not do a lot of digging into the details of an issue, but if you become their target, you can be sure they will try to do whatever it takes to make you look bad, all for the sake of a more interesting story and higher ratings.

Over the years we have has had the opportunity to work with two clients who found themselves targets of one such investigative showman. Ironically, the story itself was almost identical in both cases, as were the reporter's tactics and eventual on-air presentation. Both clients were CEOs who headed very troubled companies. One was already in bankruptcy. With the full knowledge and approval of their boards of directors, both were routinely using company aircraft for personal trips or for business travel that could have been accomplished using commercial flights. This is hardly unusual in the corporate world, but it is always catnip for this investigative reporter, who had made his reputation in several local markets by embarrassing corporate chiefs he accused of living high off the hog while their companies struggled and workers and shareholders suffered.

The reporter and his crew staked out the airfield to get tele-photo shots of company planes coming and going. He ambushed his targets on the street and at public events and chased them to their weekend homes demanding on-camera explanations of their extravagant travel practices. As could be expected, the stories he produced were short on substance but rich in theater. His objective was not so much to make news as to make his targets look bad. Until we got involved and helped our clients deal with the situation strategically, he largely succeeded. It is impossible to make investigative reporters like this go away. Telling them off or having security hustle them out of the building only plays into their hand by giving them dramatic pictures to use. But there are ways to manage the situation that can make the best of a bad situation and avoid making an already negative story even worse.

Regardless of their assignment or specialty, all reporters are driven by deadlines. They are usually in a hurry. This is especially true for reporters working in radio, television, and other electronic media. Reporters who work for an all-news radio station or cable television channel essentially face a deadline every minute of the day. Today's powerful news-gathering and distribution technologies make instant live coverage the rule rather than the exception. Wire service reporters and other print reporters whose work is intended for a Web site or a blog face similar demands for immediate turnaround, even on complex stories that might benefit from a more thoughtful and measured approach.

Most of the reporters you are likely to encounter will be generalists rather than specialists. Even a beat reporter who regularly follows you and your issues will almost certainly know less about those subjects than you do. But, in addition to raw facts, a very important part of what reporters need from you is explanation and context. They are looking for a theme. If you aren't prepared to give it to them, someone else probably will, perhaps not in the way you would prefer.

Initially, most reporters will approach just about any story from a negative perspective. This is not because of some strange character flaw peculiar to journalists, it is just that something negative is usually more newsworthy than anything positive. When things go right it just isn't news. Something going wrong almost always is. So you should always expect reporters to be inquisitive and skeptical. Expect them to be on the lookout for anything that seems negative. Expect them always to be on the prowl for a potentially sensational story. Prepare to ignore any negativity you may encounter, and just do whatever you can to give the reporter a story that is newsworthy and that delivers your message. However it may seem during the interview itself, none of a reporter's negative energy is likely to be directed at you personally. The reporter is simply doing his job, trying to get the best story possible, making it interesting, and putting it together for publication or broadcast as quickly and completely as possible. Whether you like it or not, you are an integral part of this high-pressure, competitive process. Your job is to make that process work for you rather than against you.

Editors and Producers

Editors and producers play several important roles in a news organization. An editor is responsible for assessing the relative value of all the available stories and deciding which to cover, which to ignore, which to publish or put on the air, and which to set aside for another day. Editors are also responsible for checking finished stories for accuracy, completeness, and consistency. The editor's job is to make sure every story follows the news organization's style and complies with the law. As part of this process, an editor will often cut superfluous words and unnecessary information. He may even completely rewrite the story in order to give it greater impact or clarity. Much to the annoyance of most reporters, it is almost always an editor who writes the headline and produces the teases and promotional announcements.

No matter how crucial your interview may be to the story, once it is written or produced you have no further control over the final presentation. Reporters and editors are under no obligation to show you a finished story before it runs. If they do so, you should consider it a special courtesy that gives you an opportunity to correct factual aspects of the story only. Trying to influence the theme of a story at this point will probably turn out to be counterproductive. While it is rarely useful to get into a debate with a reporter or editor over process or interpretation, most responsible news organizations do seek and appreciate guidance with respect to the hard facts. You may not agree with a news organization's interpretation of a story, but you can safely assume that they won't want to risk a flagrant misrepresentation of the facts. So don't be shy about pointing out factual errors if you see them, but resist the temptation to get into a discussion about how the story is being covered or what subjective interpretation the publication has decided to make.

We once worked with a publicity-shy CEO who found himself the subject of an extremely negative story in a major national business publication. The story came as no surprise. Our client had long been the target of consumer activists adept at generating publicity for their point of view. The reporter had been working on the piece for several months, and we knew it was coming. When it finally did appear the CEO was furious. Needless to say, he felt the story was completely unfair and wildly inaccurate.

Fairness, of course, is subjective, but the facts are the facts. Unfortunately for the angry CEO, a very careful check of every fact in every line of the published story turned up no inaccuracies at all. The CEO was certainly entitled to dispute the magazine's opinions and interpretations, but despite his insistence, we were unable to identify a single factual error.

As is often the case in such situations, the CEO insisted on sending a sharply worded letter to the editor that took strong exception to the thrust of the story. We advised against it, pointing out that the best we could hope for in the situation would be for the magazine to print our letter, and that would just put the story back in play for another week, exposing readers to the magazine's negative allegations all over again, just in case they missed them the first time around. But CEOs are CEOs and clients are clients. So we did as we were told and reluctantly submitted the letter. Sure enough, the magazine printed it in the very next issue, right at the top of the letters page, with a picture of the CEO, no less. The CEO may have been surprised, or perhaps even gratified, that the magazine was willing to print his scorching letter, but the exercise accomplished absolutely nothing strategically. The magazine didn't apologize for any factual errors. It hadn't made any. It certainly didn't back away from its negative interpretation, even though it allowed the CEO to have his say. And I doubt seriously that the CEO's letter changed the minds of many readers. Quite the contrary. The CEO may have felt better having gotten the complaint off his chest, but from a larger strategic perspective, sending that letter to the editor was entirely counterproductive.

Publications and broadcasts with longer deadlines, such as weekly or monthly magazines, sometimes employ fact-checkers whose job is to check specific facts and verify that any direct quotations accurately reflect what was actually said to the reporter.

Television news magazines sometimes assign a producer or editor to compare raw interview transcripts with the edited sound bites used in a story in order to ensure both fairness and accuracy. It is important to remember, however, that fact-checkers are responsible only for verifying the facts. It isn't their job to reshape the theme of the story or help you take back something you wish you had never said in the first place. If the reporter misquoted you, the editor or fact-checker can make it right. If you feel your words have been taken out of context, it is probably a matter of subjective interpretation. And don't expect an editor to ever let you take back something genuinely newsworthy that you have already said on camera or on the record.

7 /

Meeting the Media

How to Prepare for an Interview

I f you are asked to do a media interview, you will have an opportunity to inform and persuade an audience that might grow into the many millions. Or, at the other extreme, a strategically orchestrated media interview might allow you to communicate directly with the precise audience you need to reach. Regardless of the size of the audience or the nature of the medium, following a few basic rules will help you keep control, stay confident, and take full advantage of whatever media opportunities come your way.

Above all, you have to be prepared.

No matter how much you think you know about the subject at hand, you should never try to wing it during an interview. You will almost certainly end up crash-landing. Whether you have ten minutes or ten hours to get ready for an interview, use the time wisely to work through the strategic message development process, gather your facts, decide what you want to accomplish, and focus on the main point you want to make. Making educated guesses about what questions a reporter might ask and having good answers ready to deliver is important, but it isn't nearly enough. A successful interview is less about answering a reporter's questions than about delivering your message. Just answering questions may help the reporter, but it won't necessarily help you control the interview or shape the story around your message. Having all the answers is fine, but it prepares you only for the defensive side of the game. Answering a reporter's questions is only the first step. To be really effective in a media interview you need to have a point to make and the discipline to make it, no matter in what direction the questioning may go.

Understand Your Objective

Your mission is always to deliver a strategically important message to a carefully defined target audience. Your goal is not just to deflect the reporter's tough questions. And despite what you may think, reporters don't come looking for interviews in order to make you look bad by asking you embarrassing questions in front of thousands of people. Reporters really aren't out to ruin your day. In fact, while it may be hard to believe, reporters most of the time aren't even trying to get answers to specific questions. They probably have most of the specific information already. The question-and-answer process is a means to an end for the reporter just as it is for you. First and foremost, a reporter wants to get a good story. For a working reporter everything else is secondary. Asking tough questions is simply their way of trying to get you to make news. With this in mind, you can help yourself and the reporter by deliberately going beyond just answering questions. You should use the interview to tell a great story, one that just happens to be built around the point you want to make.

Keep It Simple

Few in the audience are likely to remember more than one or two points, no matter how many you try to make in any one interview. So it stands to reason that the fewer points you try to make, the better the odds are that the audience will remember them. To be effective in an interview you first need to focus. Regardless of what the reporter may ask, you need to decide ahead of time what you want to say, the single most important thing you want your target audience to remember. That's your key message. That's the point you want to make. And making that point is your most important objective in the interview. Everything else is just a response to the reporter's questions, important as that may be to preserving and enhancing your overall credibility. Furthermore, in order to make your point credible and memorable you need to focus on the two or three most effective pieces of evidence you can use to support it. Set everything else aside. Remember the message pyramid and try to avoid the temptation to tell the reporter everything you know about the subject at hand. Trying to say too much in an interview will only make it more difficult for you to make your point.

The Interview Process

Only a small part of what you say to a reporter is ever likely to appear in the final story, but your explanations and amplifications may still help the reporter more fully understand the issue and better appreciate your point of view. What you say may ultimately be expressed in the reporter's own words, with or without attribution to you. If your words are compelling and memorable, the reporter is more likely to pay attention, and your message is more likely to become part of the story and thereby reach your target audience. Properly handled, a media interview should always be considered an opportunity rather than a threat. Dealing with the media should never be seen as a defensive exercise. Your goal should always be to keep control of the situation so you can use the opportunity an interview offers to deliver your message to your target audience in a way that increases the odds they will remember it.

A production team from *60 Minutes* once approached one of our clients with an interesting request that illustrates quite clearly how a high-stakes media interview can be a golden opportunity rather than a potential threat. Our client was the industry leader in a very complex and controversial technology. The company's biggest challenge was to deal with charges from activist groups that their products were a danger to health and safety. Meanwhile, the *60 Minutes* producers had a problem of their own. The new technology was starting to attract a lot of attention, and they were anxious to do a story about it, but they were struggling with how to explain to a general audience just how it worked. They could have turned to the opposition and let them explain in their own terms how the new technology our client had developed was a threat to life as we know it on the planet. But even though that would have made for an interesting story, the producers understood that strident activists are not always the most credible sources of scientific information.

Given the growing controversy and the emotions involved, our client might easily have decided to turn down the *60 Minutes* interview request and let their side of the story be told by the correspondent using whatever materials the producers could dig up on their own. But sensing an opportunity, we suggested an alternative approach. We recommended that our client not only grant *60 Minutes* the interview they wanted with the company CEO, but offer them access to the company's laboratories and scientists as well. We recommended that our client offer to show *60 Minutes* the technology and discuss it on camera with the scientists who were working with it every day. We figured that this would at least give us a chance to explain the new technology in positive terms before the activists had their opportunity to condemn it. We were betting that if *60 Minutes* wanted the story badly enough and we could use our expertise to help them tell it, both of us would come out ahead and our activist opponents would be left hollering in the wilderness. They would get their share of airtime to respond, but we would get to shape the story.

We worked with the CBS producers for months, helping them understand how the technology worked and arranging to let them videotape in the laboratories. We carefully prepared the CEO and a senior scientist for their on-camera interviews. In order to measure how our messaging worked, we arranged to have a focus group watch the segment as it went on the air live and then explored their reaction in depth when it was over. The results surpassed our greatest expectations. The story was no puff piece. Our flamboyant activist opponents were given more than their share of airtime, and all aspects of the controversy were covered thoroughly. But the overall theme of the piece was the wonder of the new technology, not its potential risks. The person who was called upon to explain how it all worked was one of our client's top scientists. The person called upon to defend the industry was our client's CEO. Understanding the rules of the game and being prepared to play by them opened up a rare opportunity to reach a huge audience through a respected news organization.

Your Mission

Whatever the medium, and however large or small the audience, your job as a communicator is always to get that audience to listen and pay attention to what you have to say. It is your job to get those people to believe you, to remember your message, and to act on it. None of this will ever be easy or automatic, no matter how important you believe your message to be. Getting a message across through the media requires careful attention to a lot of important details. Bringing off that *60 Minutes* interview took the better part of a year. Preparing for that kind of high-stakes media encounter requires thoughtful attention well before you sit down for the actual interview. But if you manage to make the audience pay attention, believe what you say, and remember it long enough to take action, you will have fulfilled your strategic communications mission. Doing the interview will have been a very worthwhile exercise. You will have made your point and done your job.

Getting the audience to pay attention is becoming harder and harder every day. Even reporters, who are paid to ask questions and listen to the answers, have increasingly short attention spans. Unless you grab the reporter's attention and engage his interest early in the interview, you are likely to be disappointed with the ultimate outcome. Reporters are, however, always on the lookout for interesting stories. So, as you prepare for an interview, think carefully about how to make your message newsworthy and memorable for both the reporter and the audience, by framing it as a compelling story.

In any communications encounter, credibility is your most valuable, and most fragile, asset. We are living in a skeptical age. Just because what you have to say is true, and just because you are absolutely convinced of its importance, you can never assume that the reporter or the audience will automatically believe you. In addition to marshaling the most powerful and relevant factual evidence to support your message, you must make absolutely sure that you never do anything, consciously or unconsciously, to undermine your personal or professional credibility. If the audience you need to reach has any reason to question your honesty or your reputation, they are almost certain to doubt anything you say, even if you can prove it to be absolutely true. In the real world, emotions and impressions matter as much or more than verifiable facts. Who you are and who the audience perceives you to be matter as much or more than the factual evidence you cite to support the story you want to tell.

Finally, it doesn't matter how credible and compelling your message may be if the audience can't remember it. As you prepare for an interview think carefully about how to make your message memorable. Think about how to make your point stand out from the background noise. Think carefully about how you want your audience to respond, what you want them to do, and how the message you plan to deliver during the interview will encourage them to do it.

Thanks to the explosion of news outlets we discussed in the previous chapter, especially on the broadcast side, the odds of being asked to do an interview are increasing every day. If you are considered a good interview, media outlets probably will come back to you as often as they can. If you don't measure up, they are likely to turn to others, including those who may be antagonistic to your position. This has nothing to do with which side of an issue you happen to represent. News organizations are usually looking for a wide spectrum of opinion. It makes the story more interesting. Being a good interview is about how interesting you are, how well you are able to make your point, and whether what you have to say is newsworthy and memorable.

Interview Requests

The initial request for an interview will probably come in the form of a telephone call or e-mail from a reporter, an editor, or a producer. Make no commitments in the initial phone call. Don't immediately agree to sit for an interview. Don't promise anything but a timely return phone call. Say as little as possible. Listen as much as possible. Remember, even at the very earliest stages of reporting, nothing is ever really off the record. Anything you say to a reporter or producer, even during this initial phone call, could easily end up being used in a story. And it is always a good idea to get a phone number and call back to verify that the caller is legitimate. Just because someone says they are from *60 Minutes* or *Dateline* doesn't mean they really are.

Try to determine whether the caller is a full-time staff member or a freelancer and whether this is an assigned story or something the producer is pitching to the news outlet in the hope that it might be assigned. To a certain extent, every story under consideration by a news organization is speculative until it actually appears. Far more stories are considered than are ever actually published or broadcast. But a story being pushed by a freelancer has far less chance of making the cut than one being researched by a staff member on assignment.

If the call comes from a broadcast outlet, take note of whether the person who calls is a senior player, such as a staff producer, or someone more junior, such as a researcher or production assistant. At the big broadcast news organizations, research for major stories, especially preliminary phone calling, is often handled by junior people. But if the call comes from someone higher up in the organization, you can assume that the story is a lot further along in what is frequently a lengthy reporting and production process.

Try to determine if the news organization has already decided to do the story whether you cooperate or not, or are they still in the exploratory stage, trying to decide whether there is really a story to tell and, if so, what direction it might take. What does the news organization want from you? Are they looking for background information, clarification, a quote, an on-camera interview? Are they on deadline? How long before you have to get back to them? This is especially important for smaller, local news outlets that may have only a few hours to put a story together before broadcast.

Also try to learn how the story came to the news organization's attention. For example, did they come up with the story idea on their own, or is the story being promoted by an individual or group opposed to you or your organization? What is the initial angle or theme of the story? Who is the reporter on the story? How much time does he want to spend with you? Is he a generalist or a specialist? What has he written about you or your organization in the past? What is his reporting style? Some reporters are deliberately aggressive and provocative. Others are more low-key. Before sitting down for an interview, it helps to know as much as you can about the personal style of the reporter you will be facing. And just because a reporter may have been tough on you or your organization in the past, or even shown what you consider to be outright bias, doesn't necessarily mean that you shouldn't do the interview. You need to gather and digest as much background information as possible before making that strategic decision.

The news organization is under no obligation to give you any of this information of course, but neither are you under any obligation to make yourself available for an interview. You should always ask yourself whether doing this interview with this news organization will help you make your point to your target audience. Will this interview help you reach your strategic objective? Whether to do an interview is a strategic decision that should always be based on a careful assessment of the potential risks and benefits.

After the initial contact is made, radio and television producers often ask to do a preinterview during which they will try out possible questions and explore in more depth your position on the issue at hand. Like you, they want the actual interview to go smoothly. They want to avoid any surprises that might ruin a live appearance or waste the time and money they are investing in a taped interview. In some instances, the preinterview may even serve to disqualify a potential interview subject, either because their answers turn out not to be what the news organization expected, or because their delivery is not up to standard.

Assuming you pass this initial test, the preinterview can be a valuable opportunity for you to get a sense of what the reporter is really looking for. It allows you to try out the message you hope to deliver and gauge the reaction. You may even have a chance to suggest specific questions that you are well prepared to answer. Therefore, before you agree to a preinterview you should be well along in the development of your message. After the preinterview you will be in a much better position to refine that message, and your responses to anticipated questions, in light of what you've learned about how the reporter or producer is planning to proceed.

To Speak or Not to Speak

In today's saturated media environment, keeping silent usually sends the negative message that you have nothing worthwhile to say, or worse, that you have something embarrassing to hide. If you fail to seize every available opportunity to tell your story as you want it told, you can be sure that others will be eager to tell it for you. You may not like it, but agreeing to an interview, even under difficult circumstances, is usually the best course of action. Refusing to be interviewed will never keep a reporter from doing the story. Indeed, it may actually increase the reporter's curiosity and thereby attract more negative attention. Your unwillingness to tell your side of the story makes it more likely that your position will receive less attention and less positive exposure, leaving the field wide open for the opposition.

While merely talking to a reporter can never guarantee that the final story will be positive, or even that your message will make the cut, it does at least assure that your position and point of view are in play. Whether we like it or not, human nature dictates that unfounded rumors and gossip will always rush in to fill any communications vacuum. You cannot control what others say about you, but, by taking advantage of the opportunity to deliver your message in your own words, you can at least control what you say for yourself. While there is no way to guarantee that the reporter will use your message, taking advantage of the opportunity to put it on the record improves the odds to no worse than fifty-fifty. That's a lot better than no chance at all.

Just because a reporter or producer appears friendly and cooperative does not mean you can relax. It may just be an act aimed at getting you to say something that isn't really helpful to you strategically. On the other hand, just because a reporter seems to be uncooperative doesn't necessarily mean you shouldn't try to be helpful. Your only concern should be whether the proposed interview will give you a reasonable opportunity to make your point. That's all that matters to you from a strategic point of view.

Getting Quoted

Regardless of the medium in which they work, reporters are always looking for good quotes. Often, the primary purpose of an interview is just to put your quote on the record. The rest of the story may already be finished. But if the reporter comes across a great quote or sound bite, he may still shift gears and write around that interesting quote, even if it is not exactly the angle he originally planned to use. If you are able to deliver a memorable quote that effectively makes your point, you will have a much better chance of shaping the story as a whole. Most quotes, broadcast or print, are short. Long and involved explanations may educate an interested reporter, but they are unlikely ever to appear in the final story and therefore won't ever reach your target audience.

For example, if you were the head of a troubled automobile company and a reporter were to ask you about upheaval in your senior management ranks, you might be tempted to explain the situation in some detail:

> Our new head of marketing set records for sales growth at Jones Motors, and our new production chief cut costs by 20 percent when he was at Lasagna Automotive. Since I came to Smith Motors last year, we have recruited senior executives from across the automobile industry, people with a wide range of skills and many years of experience in all aspects of our business. We are aggressively retooling our executive ranks because to make our turnaround plan work we need experienced and dedicated people throughout the organization, but especially working with me in senior management.

That quote takes about thirty-five seconds to say, and would be difficult for a reporter, especially a television or radio reporter, to trim down to a usable length. But the key point could be made quite clearly in less than ten seconds.

In order to turn this company around we need to recruit the best people we can find, anywhere we can find them. And that's exactly what we're doing.

You can still add some supporting evidence, but only after you have offered the reporter the short, usable sound bite that makes your point.

For example, our new head of marketing set records for sales growth at Jones Motors, and our new production chief cut costs by 20 percent when he was at Lasagna Automotive.

Using the message pyramid will help you focus and refine your message and make your point with a memorable quote.

It may surprise you to learn that a reporter's first priority is not to make you look bad. Quite to the contrary, the reporter has a vested interest in helping you look intelligent and articulate. The better you are, the better the story will be. The more intelligent you sound, the more intelligent the reporter will look. Stumbles and embarrassing quotes rarely appear in print or on the air. The one important exception to this rule is the clever but inappropriate reply or the sudden lapse in memory or judgment that instantly becomes a news story in itself. And of course, an investigative reporter may try to generate some fresh news by catching you in a lie, an inconsistency, or an on-camera confession. But most reporters are just out to get a good story and tell it in a way that their readers and viewers will understand. If your message is positive, well prepared, and well delivered, you and your organization will look good, or at least as good as possible under the circumstances. Even if you avoid making any serious mistakes, but because of a lack of preparation or disciplined delivery, manage only to spend the limited time an interview offers fending off the reporter's negative questions, you may not do any damage to your cause, but you will have missed a valuable strategic opportunity.

Hard news coverage looks for conflict and highlights the unusual. A reporter is simply doing his job when he reports on sensational or conflict-oriented situations, whatever their broader importance may be. Good reporters are always on the lookout for conflict, controversy, winners and losers, victims and villains. These are what make good stories, and a good story is what the reporter came to get. In the absence of genuine conflict a reporter may even try to get you to say something that will get you into a fight. Don't fall for it. Always remember your strategic mission and the point you want to make. Never let a reporter's attempt to get you to "commit news" on his terms distract you from your effort to make your point in a way that the audience will remember.

An interview opportunity can also be used to cultivate a long-term relationship with a reporter or producer. In many cases, the story that attracted the reporter to you in the first place will be based on bad news or problems that you would rather not see publicized. But if you deliver a good interview under difficult circumstances, the reporter may come back to you later for a story you actually want to see covered. If you turn out to be a bad interview, the reporter may never call again, and you will miss future opportunities for positive media exposure. It makes sense to be as good as you can be in every interview, even when the short-term payoff is likely to be limited.

Especially when doing broadcast interviews, brevity is important. Most people routinely speak at a rate of about 150 words per minute. The average quote or sound bite today is less than ten seconds. That boils down to about twenty-five words. Make every one count. Even on the Web, where space and time are of little concern, your initial quote is likely to be brief, with an embedded link to a longer version, full text, background material, and additional links to related stories and other sites. But unless your quote jumps off the screen and grabs the reader's attention instantly, few will bother to click the link to read any further. It would be the online equivalent of a radio or television sound bite that is so long and complicated that it never gets used in the final story. The sound bite is to a broadcast news story what the direct quotation is to a newspaper article. Regardless of the medium, you aren't telling the story, the reporter is. What the reporter wants from you is a memorable quote that cuts to the heart of the issue, a memorable quote that sums up your position, a memorable quote that brings your message to life for the audience. In order to make sure that what you say during the interview makes it into the story, you need to make your point clearly, colorfully, and in better words than the reporter could find for himself. Given the increasing brevity of both print and broadcast stories and the likelihood that you will not be the only source interviewed for the story, you can usually expect to be on the air or quoted in the newspaper for only about one short sentence. Decide in advance what you want your target audience to remember and then focus all your efforts during the interview on making sure they do.

Taking Control

It may seem like a tall order at first, but in order for a media interview to advance your strategic agenda, you must take control. You have to make it your interview as much as it is the reporter's. This is never easy of course, but it is far from impossible, thanks to a few simple techniques you can learn and practice well before you sit down for an interview. It is perfectly natural to be nervous about possibly saying something inappropriate or forgetting to say something you planned to get across during an interview. The best way to deal with that kind of nervousness is to prepare thoroughly by deciding ahead of time what key points you want to make and how you want to make them. This will minimize the chance of saying something foolish, or forgetting to say what is most important.

If possible, send the reporter a one-page fact sheet and supporting material before the interview, and keep a copy for yourself. This summary should include basic facts and figures relevant to the story, a brief description of your organization, a quick review of the issues, and a short personal biography. The shorter the better. Don't bother sending your company's latest annual report. Background information is very useful to the reporter, but few interviewers have time to read lengthy material, no matter how important. Putting together this brief backgrounder will help the reporter, but it will also help you by forcing you to focus on what is most important.

Know exactly what you want to say before the reporter ever walks through the door. Have your message well prepared and firmly in mind. Imagine what you would like to see when the story finally appears. How would you write the story if you had the opportunity? How would you like to be quoted? What headline would you use? If you don't say something, the reporter can't possibly use it, so try to get your message into the interview as early and as often as possible. And never be afraid to repeat your main point at every reasonable opportunity. The more often you make your point, the more likely the reporter will be to use it. Remember, you are the expert. Even if a reporter knows nothing about the issue or is openly hostile to your position going in, they can still come away from the interview with your message on the record.

If the interview starts out with a series of friendly warm-up questions, don't be lulled into a false sense of security. Reporters generally begin this way just to gather basic information and get you relaxed and talking freely. Don't let your attention wander. Never drop your guard at any time during the interview. Take advantage of a friendly question to deliver your key message early in the interview. If your message is clear, strong, and well framed it might lead the reporter down a road you want him to travel and discourage him from raising issues that would be harder for you to deal with.

Remember that anything and everything you say before, after, as well as during an interview, with or without a camera or tape recorder rolling, is on the record and may be used in the final story. We once worked with a corporate executive who after a tough day of meetings in Washington got into what he assumed was a casual conversation with another passenger on the shuttle flight back to New York. Our client never bothered to ask the other passenger what he did for a living, and the other passenger never volunteered. He didn't take notes. He didn't ask tough questions. He just listened politely as our client described in some detail the problems he and his company were having with federal regulators. Imagine our client's surprise when he saw what he said mentioned in the next morning's paper. Reporters ride airplanes, too, and anything you say to anyone might find its way into a news story.

If the reporter seems to be engaging in idle chatter before an interview, it may be nothing more than that, but it may also be a deliberate tactic the reporter is using to take your measure and decide what lines of questioning to pursue and how. This is a very good time to deliver your message in the hope that it will steer the reporter in a direction you want him to go. Just because a reporter doesn't appear to be taking notes doesn't mean that he won't remember what you say and use it in a story. A clever reporter will usually wait until the very end of an interview to ask the tough, accusatory questions, just in case you get angry and refuse to continue. If this happens, never lose control, no matter how aggressive the reporter may act. Never demand that the interview be stopped. If that happens on camera, it makes great television, but terrible public relations. Indeed, your outburst could very easily become the main theme of the reporter's story, and if that happens, you will have utterly failed to achieve your strategic objective. The positive message you came to deliver will get pushed far into the background or out of the story altogether.

Answering Questions

If you are well prepared you will be able to answer even the toughest questions. Using bridging words will help you work your key message into your answers, no matter how rambling, aggressive, or antagonistic the reporter's question may sound. Remain calm and centered. If you keep in mind at all times why you are doing the interview in the first place, you will be able to relax and engage the reporter, no matter how difficult he or she may seem at first. Get to the point you want to make as quickly as possible. If you make it too difficult for the reporter to find your message, he may not bother to try, or may pick out a less important message from everything you say. Either way, you will have lost an important opportunity to make your point.

Consider the following example of how you might handle a potentially difficult question:

Question: Does your company test the dolls you make to see if button eyes might come off and be swallowed by children playing with them?

Weak Answer: Yes.

Better Answer: Yes, we do. It's a matter of the highest priority to see that our dolls are safe. Safe toys are more than just good business. Making safe dolls is part of our social responsibility. Our own kids love dolls, too.

Accusatory Question: When is your company going to stop making unsafe dolls that kill helpless children?

Good Answer: Safety is our number-one priority. Safe toys are more than just good business for Dolls, Incorporated. Making safe dolls is part of our social responsibility. We spend more than a hundred thousand dollars a year testing our dolls to make sure they are safe. Most of us here have kids of our own at home, and we give them our company's dolls to play with. That tells you how safe we think our products are.

It shouldn't matter to you whether the reporter poses the question gently or aggressively. All the questions in this example are about exactly the same issue, safety. If you have done your homework and prepared thoroughly for the interview, you will know in advance that safety is a topic you are likely to be asked about. You will have prepared a response about safety and will be ready to deliver it as soon as you identify the broad category into which the reporter's specific question falls. The most effective way to deliver your message is always to stay positive and proactive, regardless of the reporter's attitude. An interview is not a duel. Arguing with the reporter won't help to get your message to the audience. You can never win an argument with a reporter. In the end, they always get to write the story.

Controlling the Interview

Answering the doll safety question with a simple yes would have been perfectly accurate, of course. But accuracy alone is never enough. You didn't agree to be interviewed just to answer the reporter's questions and convey factual information he could more easily have gathered for himself on the Internet. That puts all the control in the reporter's hands. You are doing the interview in order to deliver your message about your company's devotion to doll safety to a strategically important target audience. This is your interview, too, and you must seize the opportunity it offers to go beyond simple answers and deliver your key message in a way that will help the audience remember and act on it.

While you should always strive for a relaxed, conversational delivery, a media interview is never just an ordinary conversation. Although effective responses to the reporter's direct questions are an absolute prerequisite for effective message delivery, your ultimate objective is not just to answer questions. Your mission is to deliver a message. The reporter's mission is to get a good story. Framing your message as a compelling story is usually more effective than making the reporter force it out of you or figure it out for himself.

If you help the reporter get a good story, he is more likely to help you make your point.

The target audience you are trying to reach is more likely to remember what you say if you use words and concepts that are easily understandable to the general public. Avoid jargon. Never use fancy words when simple ones will do as well. In a story about a real estate dispute you could answer: "Notwithstanding allegations to the contrary, we maintain that the ownership of the real property in question, corporeal and incorporeal combined, is vested with our corporation." But it would be a lot more effective just to translate it into plain English and say: "Our company owns the land." In the Dolls, Incorporated example, it would have been perfectly accurate to talk about "stress testing and repetitive simulations of all possible abuse situations." But it would be much more effective to describe the testing process as "putting Raggedy Andy in the clutches of a machine that beats up on him like five hundred four-year-olds."

Even though we understand that a successful interview is never just about answering questions, under the pressure of a real interview situation, it is easy to fall into the trap of seeing the questioner as a teacher asking tough questions and expecting fast, accurate answers. Instinct and years of practice lead us to believe that if we just answer the reporter's questions quickly, accurately, and without saying anything harmful or embarrassing, the interview will be a success. Nothing could be further from the truth. The reporter is not your target audience. The reporter is not your teacher. The reporter is just a newsperson looking for a good story. You are not the student. You are not doing the interview just to answer the reporter's questions. You are doing the interview in order to make an important strategic point to a well-defined target audience, an audience you hope to reach through the news outlet the reporter represents. Even under the most difficult circumstances, a media interview should always be mutually beneficial. An interview should belong to you every bit as much as it belongs to the reporter. But for that to happen you have to stay in control.

Keeping Cool Under Fire

No matter how confrontational a reporter may try to be, never allow yourself to be put on the defensive by a hostile question or one that is based on a false premise. Getting angry just increases the odds that you will commit news in a way that won't advance your strategic objective. Strange as it may seem, hostile and false premise questions are actually some of the easiest from which to bridge to a positive key message. All you need to say is "No," or "That's not true," or "I wouldn't characterize it that way," and then move on immediately to what *is* true: your key message. But always remember President Nixon's "I am not a crook" mistake and be careful never to repeat the questioner's negative words in your answer. It just makes you look defensive.

If you find yourself getting angry during a difficult interview, pause, take a deep breath, and say you want to check something you just said. Glance down for a moment. During this brief break in the action keep silent, collect your thoughts, and regain control of your emotions. Then look up and say, "Now, would you mind repeating what you were just asking?" This creates a slight delay, breaking the hostile interviewer's stride and allowing you to settle down and regain control. Whenever you find yourself in a hostile or confrontational situation, always keep your strategic mission uppermost in mind. Never allow yourself to worry so much about killing the alligators that you forget that your mission is to drain the swamp. Never take a reporter's nasty questions personally. Above all, stick to the point you want to make. Your key message is the one part of the interview that you can absolutely control, no matter what.

Multiple Questions

A reporter who is unfamiliar with the subject or who is just fishing for a story, may resort to asking you unnecessarily complex, multiple questions, hoping something in your answer will turn out to be a good quote. Multipart questions can be very confusing, especially if you try to remember every one of the questions the reporter throws out and then try diligently to answer each one in order. When confronted with a multiple question, it is much safer and far more effective to select the one part of the question that most closely relates to your key message and then answer it, ignoring the rest. If that isn't really what the reporter is looking for, he can ask again. But in the meantime you have probably saved yourself and the reporter a lot of time and potential confusion.

What to Avoid

As part of the message development process, you have already identified questions you know you are likely to be asked but which for some good reason you should not attempt to answer. There is, of course, no magic formula that will keep a reporter from asking you these difficult questions. You can't make them go away, so you need to plan carefully for how you will handle them. The worst time to realize that you shouldn't be getting near a particular question is when you are halfway through answering it and the camera is rolling. The largest category of questions you must avoid are those for which you don't have an answer. If you don't know the answer to a question, just say so and then offer to get back to the reporter with more complete information. If the question is completely outside your area of expertise or responsibility, offer to refer the reporter to a better-informed source. The reporter will have no choice but to take you at your word and move on.

The reporter may still try to catch you off guard by encouraging you to speculate, often by posing a hypothetical question:

> Well, Mr. Jones, I understand that you still don't know exactly what caused the explosion, but do you think it might have been a slow leak from that big methyl isocyanate tank over there? That's what one expert we've spoken with thinks happened.

Don't take the bait. Your speculation, however reasonable and helpful it may seem at the time, could turn out to be all wrong. And, of course, you have no way of knowing if the reporter has really talked to any "expert" at all. When faced with a *what if?* question, have the discipline to respond only with *what is,* what you know to be the verifiable facts. Then immediately bridge to the point you want to make.

> The cause of this explosion is still a mystery. We're working day and night to get to the bottom of it. But what's most important right now is the health and safety of our workers and everyone who lives near the plant. Here's what we're doing about that . . .

Your answer begins with a polite refusal to speculate about the cause of the blast. Then it moves on to the point you want to make about the importance of health and safety, followed by specific information that illustrates what you are doing to follow through. Similarly, if the reporter brings up pending litigation, trade secrets, personnel matters, security issues, or any other forbidden area, you should resist the temptation to start down a dangerous path by offering hints or partial answers. Just move quickly to what you are able to talk about freely: your key message, the point you want to make. Some examples of how to deflect forbidden questions:

> I'm afraid it's a bit too early to talk about that now. I'll have to wait until all the tests are completed. But in the meantime, I can tell you that we are . . .

> I'm sure you know that our competitors would really like to have that information, too, so you can certainly understand why I can't give it to you now.

> The pending court case makes it impossible for me to discuss the plaintiff's allegations. But I can tell you that our tests have shown this product to be safe when properly applied, and beyond that, we have a record of safety that is the envy of the industry.

The reporter may very well come back at you several times with the same question in a slightly different form, hoping that you will slip up and speculate on the record. But eventually, if you make it clear you are not going to go down that road and are able to clearly and credibly explain why, you'll leave the reporter with no choice but to move on. Being able to explain clearly why you can't answer makes you look reasonable and credible. Just refusing to respond makes you look arrogant and guilty. And even the slightest speculation about something negative can easily lead you down a dangerous path toward repeating the negative speculation, even as you are trying to refute it.

You can also control the flow and outcome of an interview by paying close attention to the overall nature of the reporter's questions. If you are asked a *macro* question: "What is the meaning of life?" consider focusing your answer on the *micro* point you most want to make: "Life for this company is mostly about making safer dolls." If you are asked a micro question: "Exactly how many angels can dance on the head of a pin?" consider giving a macro answer: "Let me explain why angels dancing on the heads of pins matter so much to our company in the first place." The reporter gets to ask the questions. But doesn't get to control the answers, unless you allow it.

If you clearly understand your strategic objective and come to the interview well prepared with a memorable point to make, you will be able to deliver it in a newsworthy fashion right off the bat. The reporter won't be forced to send out a search party to find your message in a blizzard of mostly extraneous information. If you have a good story to tell and are prepared to tell it in a way that helps the reporter do his job, he won't feel the need to trap you with hypothetical questions, or make you angry, or try to catch you off base in order to get a good story, a story that includes a memorable quote that makes your point.

Off the Record

It is often said that a secret is something you tell people one at a time. When dealing with the news media it is a good idea to keep that somewhat cynical observation in mind. Despite what you may have been told, nothing you say to any reporter is ever really "off the record," at least not for very long. No matter how well you know a reporter and no matter how hard that reporter may push you for information "on background," be careful. If a reporter fails to live up to his side of the bargain, you don't ever have to talk to him again. But by that time, whatever you said has probably been published, and you may already be looking for a new line of work. Never assume that you can make an unbreakable "off the record" deal with a real reporter. There is just too much opportunity for legitimate misunderstanding, not to mention outright deception. You have no way of knowing whether the reporter has permission from his editor or publisher to make such a deal in the first place. You have no way of knowing whether a judge or special prosecutor may some day compel the reporter to reveal your name or risk going to jail to protect their confidential source. Rather than engaging in complex negotiations over what will be on or off the record, it is usually better to assume (and make clear to the reporter up front) that he is free to use anything you say. Then discipline yourself never to say anything before, during, or after an interview that you wouldn't feel perfectly comfortable seeing published or broadcast the next day. This not only gives a valuable boost to your overall credibility, but also gives you an additional incentive to think very carefully about exactly what you want to say before you say it. Just another example of how you can advance your strategic agenda by helping the reporter do his job.

No Comment

"No comment" is never a useful response. Your motives for refusing to answer a particular question may be entirely honest and innocent, but if you respond to a reporter's question with anything resembling "no comment," the audience will assume that you have something to hide. Unfortunately, using a phrase like "no comment" is very much like invoking your constitutional rights under the Fifth Amendment. It may be perfectly legal and perhaps even honorable and justified under the circumstances. But it is almost certainly a losing strategy in the unforgiving court of public opinion. Luckily, there are other ways to say essentially the same thing without damaging your credibility:

> We find the allegations "interesting," but that's all I can say for the moment.

> That deals with only one aspect of a much larger issue.

> That is just one of the things we have under study right now. *(Then give a lengthy account of something else that you have "under study" that reflects better upon your organization.)*

This is really just another form of bridging, and the key, as always, is to anticipate and prepare. None of these tools and techniques is likely to work very well if you try to use them on the fly. Under the pressure of a real interview, it is just too easy to default to the familiar question-and-answer mode, leaving the reporter in charge of asking the tough questions and you in the uncomfortable position of giving the best defensive answers you can come up with at the time. Thoughtful and efficient preparation will help put you back in control of the interview process and make it a lot easier for you to tell your story to your target audience, no matter what questions the reporter may ask or how he may ask them.

Honesty

No matter how uncomfortable the circumstances, honesty is always the best policy. If you ever fail to tell a reporter the whole truth, and your deception is later discovered, you could very well end up as the subject of a much bigger, very ugly, and entirely avoidable story. Whatever the story may have been originally, your false statement will quickly become the new headline, and your credibility will be permanently damaged. As they say in Washington, the biggest scandals are more often about the cover-up than the original crime. I. Lewis "Scooter" Libby was never prosecuted for the underlying crime of revealing the name of a covert CIA operative. The special prosecutor decided early in his investigation that there was insufficient evidence to prove the charge. But Libby was eventually convicted of lying in order to cover up what he apparently thought was a serious crime. The best way to preserve your credibility is to prepare for the interview by anticipating the toughest possible questions and working through the answers in advance, making absolutely sure that anything you say will be absolutely accurate.

Humor

Humor is great, but only if you can pull it off without generating unexpected antagonism or seeming to make light of an unpleasant situation. The ability to tell funny jokes is a gift. Most people just don't have it, and there is nothing worse than a joke that falls flat. It is usually best to avoid trying to be humorous altogether, but if you must, always try out your jokes in advance on someone you know doesn't have a great sense of humor, someone with no vested interest in your success as an amateur comedian. If that humorless person reacts well, it might be safe to try the line during an interview. But you still need to handle humor with great care. Just because your friends and colleagues tell you your jokes are hilarious doesn't guarantee that an audience of outsiders will agree.

When he was CEO of the Walt Disney Company, Michael Eisner once appeared on NBC's *Today* show to talk about Disney's new animal park in Florida. Unlike most of Disney's theme park exhibits, this park featured lots of live animals, and it quickly became the subject of a raging controversy that pitted the company against animal rights activists. *Today* was broadcasting live from the new animal park on opening day. It was strictly a promotional exercise. It wasn't a hard-hitting investigative report. But when it came time for Eisner's live interview, his performance was very strange indeed. After weeks of controversy, Eisner came to the interview with an obviously defensive, even hostile, attitude. He made it abundantly clear just how annoyed he was that anyone would possibly question his company's good intentions. It was obvious that he was feeling the heat generated by the animal rights protestors, and he obviously wasn't well prepared to deal with the inescapable fact that some animals had indeed died as the park was being prepared for opening day. The latest incident involved several exotic birds that had been run over by one of the buses that would be carrying visitors through the park. The interviewer in the segment was Katie Couric, not someone known for tough interrogations, and none of her questions came close to being hostile. If Eisner had played along as the producers expected he would, the interview would have ended up as just another part of a well-orchestrated opening day promotion. But for some reason Eisner decided to make a joke about the dead animals. He went out of his way to remind a visibly surprised Couric that "every animal in this park will die eventually, and so will all of us." True enough, but under the circumstances not at all an amusing line. The joke fell flat. On the tape, Couric seems to grow increasingly uncomfortable as Eisner insists on illustrating his point by making light of dead animals and reminding everyone in the audience of their own mortality.

It is impossible to know for sure what possessed such a smart guy to do such a dumb thing on national television, but I do have a theory. Knowing that the accidental deaths of some of the animals in the new park was in the news and that the animal rights activists were already using the story in an effort to embarrass Disney, Eisner and his communications team correctly anticipated that he would get asked about it, even though the overall interview was intended to be light and promotional. During a communications strategy session someone probably made a joke about how foolish and unrealistic the animal rights activists were acting. That may have led Eisner to try out the line about dead animals on his team. Because he was the CEO, everyone probably laughed. That led Eisner to conclude, incorrectly as it turned out, that his joke about dead animals would work as well with a national television audience as it had with a bunch of Disney executives who were being paid a lot of money to say yes as soon as the boss was finished talking. That turned out to be a very bad mistake.

Numbers

Avoid using too many numbers, either on the air or in print. Especially on radio and television, numbers generally go whizzing by the audience, leaving behind more confusion than clarity. Even in newspapers and magazines, where the reader can always slow down to reread a complicated number, throwing in too many statistics makes it difficult to appreciate their individual significance. Most viewers, listeners, and even readers will probably pay close enough attention to recognize a number as being large or small. Beyond that, they are unlikely to remember precisely how big or how small. Rattling off a series of bewildering statistics, even if they are absolutely accurate and highly relevant to the subject at hand, may make the audience think you are deliberately trying to confuse them, and that will only undermine your credibility.

If you can't avoid using numbers, it often helps to round them off so they can be more easily remembered. For example, instead of saying, "1,231," say "about twelve hundred." Instead of saying, "243,350," say, "more than a quarter of a million." Instead of "999,997,542" try using "just under a billion." If you have no choice but to use very specific numbers because of the particular nature of the issue, it helps to use only one set of figures per sentence. For print media, you might provide charts and graphs to use as illustrations. But don't expect a television crew to take pictures of your charts, although they may decide to use your data to create their own graphics.

Mistakes

We all make mistakes. If it happens to you during an interview, don't fumble around trying to retrieve the correct answer. Just stop and say, "I'd like to try that again, if I may." The same applies if you suddenly realize that you made a mistake or possibly left a wrong impression earlier in the interview. Never call unwanted attention to your mistake by explaining what it was. Just pause and say, "I'd like to go back to something we dealt with earlier," and then repeat your previous answer, but this time with the correct information or emphasis. Anyone can lose his train of thought during an interview. Anyone can get flustered under tough questioning. If it starts happening to you, don't panic, just try one of the following techniques:

Stop and say to the reporter, "You know, I'm not sure I'm getting at what you want. Would you please rephrase the question for me?" While the reporter responds, you get some time to take a deep breath and collect your thoughts. Or stop and say, "I'd like to answer that again." Then pause, look down, and think through your specific response, your bridge phrase, and the main point you want to make before giving it another try.

If you don't understand a question, never be afraid to ask the reporter to repeat it. Never just guess and try to answer what you *think* the reporter asked. If the question is completely bewildering, or you are getting so flustered that you simply can't remember what it was, try going straight to your key message. Just make your point. The reporter may be just as confused as you are, and repeating your message may be all you need to regain control of the interview and get the reporter back on track. At the very least, you will have taken advantage of another opportunity to put your message on the record.

Keeping Pace

In an effort to throw you off your game and perhaps even get you to say something you shouldn't, a reporter may try to speed up the pace of the interview, barraging you with questions and barely giving you time to react, much less respond thoroughly and thoughtfully. If you find yourself being forced into an uncomfortable rhythm during an interview, just stop talking. All the reporter can do is pause right along with you or jump in with another question. Either way, pausing puts you back in control of the interview. Eventually the reporter will be forced to let you deliver your answers at your own pace. If the reporter continues to interrupt, you may be forced to say something like, "Please let me finish. You've asked a good question, and I want to make sure you get the answer." Always stay calm but assertive. Politely insist on making your point, even if it takes you several tries to do it. Remember, the reporter can't use what you *don't* say. But anything you *do* say could possibly be used against you. Deliberately speeding up the pace of an interview is just a reporter's trick to get you off track and perhaps make news you don't want to make.

E-mail Interviews

Many reporters now routinely put questions to their sources by e-mail. This is especially true when the reporter's questions are few and very specific. Some people even go so far as to refuse to answer questions from reporters except by e-mail, insisting on keeping a written record of exactly what was asked and exactly how they responded. Responding to a reporter's questions by e-mail can be both convenient and effective, but only if you follow the same rules of message development and delivery that you would use in a live interview. The biggest advantage of an e-mail interview, of course, is that it gives you plenty of time to consider each question and frame a careful response. The biggest risk is that you will answer the reporter's specific questions brilliantly but fail to bridge effectively to your main point. So, before replying to a reporter's e-mailed questions, take the time to craft bridges from your responses to your key message and be careful to include both in your written replies. Including your key message in your e-mailed replies to a reporter's questions will not guarantee that the reporter will use it in his story any more than it would in a live interview, but forgetting to include your message, or only offering it in response to a closely related direct question, will reduce the odds of successfully making your point to near zero.

Telephone Interviews

Print and radio reporters often contact their interview subjects by telephone. Indeed, most of the interviews you are likely to do will probably be by phone. There are some useful techniques that will help you get your message across effectively in a phone interview. When doing interviews on the phone many print reporters take notes directly on their computers. Listen carefully. While talking with the reporter you probably will be able to hear the keys tapping in the background. If you hear the reporter typing, you can assume that he is busily taking notes on what you are saying. If you have just delivered your key message, force yourself to wait until you hear the keyboard go silent before continuing to talk. Let the reporter have as much time as he needs to take down your message. That's why you decided to do the interview in the first place. Similarly, if you don't hear any tapping after you say something important, the reporter may have been distracted or may not have grasped the significance of your message. Repeat it until you are sure he has gotten the point and taken it down.

One big advantage of doing an interview on the phone is that you can lay out your notes like cue cards on your desk. You can also use notes when the reporter is physically present of course, but this is usually clumsy and distracting. It makes you look over-programmed. But during a telephone interview you can have all the notes you need arranged conveniently in front of you. You can write out all your "talking points," including well-crafted responses to the expected areas of questioning, memorable bits of supporting evidence, bridge phrases, and above all, your key message.

Recording

Many print reporters routinely tape their telephone interviews in order to make sure they don't miss anything. Common courtesy suggests that the reporter should tell you if your conversation is being recorded. In some states this is even required by law. But recognizing that anything you say to a reporter should be considered on the record, regardless of the location or circumstances, you should always assume that your interview is being recorded, whether you are specifically informed about it or not.

Federal regulations require that a licensed radio or television station get your specific permission before broadcasting anything you say on the telephone, live or recorded. But here again, it is always safer to assume that you will be going on the air, so avoid saying anything you wouldn't want to be broadcast, whether or not the reporter or producer asks your permission in advance. There are plenty of unfortunate examples of people who thought they were having a casual preliminary telephone conversation with a reporter or producer, only to discover too late that they were live on the air or were being taped for later broadcast. And once something is on tape there is no way you can ever take it back. Former Georgia congresswoman Cynthia McKinney learned this the hard way when she stormed out of a particularly contentious television interview but forgot that she was still wearing a wireless microphone. Out in the hall she berated her staff for messing up the interview, calling one of her staffers a "fool." Then she remembered the microphone and rushed back into the room demanding that anything she had said out in the hall be off the record. No such luck. Everything McKinney said to the amazed reporters was still being recorded and, of course, became the story. McKinney complained bitterly about irresponsible reporters trying to make her look bad, but she said what she said, and once it was on tape she had no choice but to take responsibility for it.

Note also that newer media outlets, such as satellite radio and Internet feeds that don't make use of the public airwaves, are not licensed by the government and are therefore not subject to the same regulations that apply to traditional radio and television broadcast stations. What might seem like a casual conversation with a blogger could easily end up being recorded and put out over the Internet where it is instantly available to the conventional news media as well as casual Web surfers. In this age of digital audio recorders and cell phone cameras, anything you say or do anywhere is now fair game for worldwide distribution.

If possible, always try to do telephone interviews standing up. Standing helps keep you alert and makes your voice sound richer and fuller. Walking around helps keep your head clear and your lungs well ventilated. If you do a lot of telephone interviews, consider equipping your phone with an extra-long handset cord or wireless headset so you can relieve tension by roaming around your office while you talk. This is especially important during long, live interviews such as radio call-in shows. Talk radio formats vary, but if you agree to appear on a call-in show it will usually be on the telephone and it may very well last for a full hour or even longer. Being able to stand up and walk around will make the experience a lot less tiring. And you will sound more alert and engaged.

Dealing with the Electronic Media

Beyond the basic considerations of message development and effective delivery that apply to any media encounter, there are a number of specific points you should keep in mind when you do live or prerecorded interviews for radio, television, or any of the so-called "new media."

Don't speak too fast, and always take a breath between sentences. Radio and television audiences need time to absorb what you say. Unlike newspaper or magazine readers, viewers and listeners can't turn back the page and reread your words. Speak clearly. Don't mumble. Higher volume can easily be cut down in the recording and editing process. But if something you say is barely audible, it is very difficult to increase the volume without distortion. Be conversational, but speak loudly enough for the reporter and the microphone to hear you clearly.

Don't step on the reporter's questions. Even if you anticipate the end of a question well before the reporter finishes asking it, resist the temptation to begin your answer before the interviewer stops speaking. Always pause for a second or two before beginning your answer. There is nothing wrong with being eager and willing to respond, but if your answer comes too close to the question (or worse, if you and the reporter are talking simultaneously for a split second) it may be impossible to edit the recording cleanly so that your answer can be used on the air. If what you say can't be used in the story, there is no point saying it in the first place.

Don't run your sentences together. Take time to pause. Pauses not only help the tape editor, they buy you time to get your thoughts together. Don't be afraid of a little bit of dead air. Well-placed pauses make your words easier to edit effectively and can also help draw attention to what comes before and after. A strategic pause that leads to a more cogent answer is well worth the time taken. The more you say, the less the audience will remember. Trying to crowd too much information into a single sound bite is counterproductive if the audience can't remember it. Better to hit the target once with a single carefully placed shot than to fire a wasteful barrage that scatters arrows all over the landscape.

Short, simple, declarative sentences may look dull on paper, but they are music to the ear. Long, complex sentences layered with dependent clauses may contain a lot of interesting information, but they are likely to obscure the clear and simple points you want your viewers and listeners to remember. Force yourself to speak in simple declarative sentences whenever possible. When you are tempted to use a compound sentence, break it into two simpler sentences for clarity.

Think About How You Sound

For many people, making *er* and *um* noises is an unconscious way of gaining breathing and thinking time in casual conversation. Unfortunately, *ums, ers,* and the like stick out like a sore thumb on the air. If you are in the habit of using a lot of these little breaks in your regular speech, take time to practice saying simple declarative sentences all the way through without pausing. Try using an inexpensive audio recorder to listen to yourself answering questions. Once you get over the shock of hearing your voice as others have always heard it, you are likely to discover some annoying speech habits you never realized you had. Habits that you probably can fix on the spot. And do try to avoid the annoying filler phrase *you know.* Most of us aren't even aware that, *you know,* we're saying *you know* at all. But the audience will definitely notice, and listeners are likely to be, *you know,* distracted from your, *you know,* key message. Again, something that most people would hardly notice or care about in casual conversation may create a serious and entirely avoidable distraction in the less forgiving environment of a broadcast interview.

Avoid Pronouns

Written prose is full of pronouns like you, they, it, and her. Pronouns serve the valuable purpose of saving space and smoothing the text for easier silent reading. But in a broadcast interview it is better to stick with nouns and proper names, even if it strikes you at first as clumsy and repetitive. Again, listeners and viewers can't go back to the tape to check an antecedent the way they can turn back the page of a newspaper. If you use too many pronouns, viewers and listeners may get confused. Whatever energy the audience is forced to spend trying to figure out which pronoun stands for which noun is energy they won't have left to process the main point you want them to remember. Moreover, when it comes time to edit your interview for broadcast, if a sentence in your answer that would be perfect for use on the air happens to contain a pronoun that refers back to something in a previous sentence, both sentences would have to be used for either to make any sense to the viewer or listener. If the reporter only has room for a single, short sound bite, your well-crafted key message might end up on the cutting room floor.

For example, suppose you were to say during an interview, "OSHA is currently conducting a lengthy study that may or may not turn up a problem with the way doll makers demand that their employees use dangerous machines to test their products.

They're on a fishing expedition. It's a waste of taxpayer money." The first sentence is rather long, so the reporter may want to deliver that information himself and then use either the second or the third sentence alone as your sound bite. But the pronouns "it" and "they" would make that impossible. Repeating the proper noun would have allowed the reporter to use either of your shorter and stronger sentences as a sound bite standing alone: "OSHA is on a fishing expedition. The OSHA study is a waste of taxpayer money." Don't risk letting the strong message you want to deliver get lost in the editing process. For the sake of clarity, impact, and ease of editing, stick to nouns.

Location

Occasionally a television reporter may invite you to a studio or ask to do an interview outdoors, but usually they will want to come to your office. Unless you have a large office with a well-appointed conversation area, you should arrange to do on-camera interviews in a conference room or other area that allows adequate space for camera placement and lighting. Avoid rooms with heat or air conditioning blowers that cannot be shut off. Carefully check your office and conference room ahead of time. You may be so used to the white noise all around you every day that you don't even realize it is there. But the microphones will pick up all that background noise and make your interview sound as if it had been recorded on a busy street during rush hour. Make certain that your office or conference room has easily accessible electrical outlets for lights and other equipment. If someone can point out the wall plugs to the camera crew as soon as they arrive, it will save a lot of time and trouble. Everyone involved will be grateful.

Always have an alternate interview site selected ahead of time. If your first choice turns out to be unsatisfactory for some unpredictable reason, you don't want to waste valuable time and energy (and increase your own nervousness) looking for a new location at the last minute. The crew will bring all the gear they need. All they require of you are a suitable location, adequate electrical outlets, and plenty of time to get everything set up.

If you are concerned about possible misquotation or out-of-context editing, you can arrange in advance to have your own audio or video recorder on hand to tape the entire interview as it is being shot. Your equipment need not interfere with the crew's gear, as long as you are careful to stay out of their way. Because it has become relatively common for subjects of major interviews to make their own recordings, many news organizations have established policies to govern the practice. Often they will ask that you sign or record a statement promising to respect the news organization's copyright and not use the recording you make for any commercial purpose. This is a perfectly reasonable request.

Quite apart from keeping a complete record of everything you were asked and everything you said in response, it is often very helpful to review your recording of the full interview later in order to analyze your performance. Did you accurately anticipate the broad areas of questioning? Did you explain complicated subjects effectively? Did you use too many *ers, ums,* and *you knows?* How long did it take you to bridge to your key message? Was your message clear, well delivered, and memorable? Was it shaped as a message pyramid?

Always record the completed story from the newscast so you can compare your original interview with what was actually used on the air. This will allow you to judge how well your message survived the editing process and help you find ways to deliver it even more effectively the next time. And of course, having a recording of the entire unedited interview, as well as the final story, also gives you the raw material you might need to demonstrate later whether any of your comments were taken out of context or otherwise distorted.

Appearance

Much has been written about how to dress for television interviews, but all that wise advice can be summed up in a single word: *distraction.* Anything you wear and anything in the way you present yourself that distracts from the message you are trying to deliver and the image you are trying to convey is bad. Everything else is just fine. Above all, don't get so wrapped up in your physical appearance that you neglect your message or distract yourself from making your point during the interview. You are not an actor playing a character. You should always strive to come across as your own honest self.

With that said, there are some simple suggestions that will help you deal with specific issues of on-air appearance and dress. For men, the best attire for television is conservative, dark business clothing. Women should wear an equivalent outfit. Don't wear clothes with small, sharply contrasting color patterns. The light will play off the pattern in a way that distracts viewers. For similar reasons, avoid loud checks and plaids. Avoid loud colors. A pale blue shirt and subdued red necktie will compliment your skin color on camera. In general, blue helps most people look their best under the lights. It is no accident that most Washington briefing rooms have blue drapes behind the podium. The government didn't get a special deal on blue cloth. It's just that most people look their best against a blue background.

Makeup

Before appearing on television or in a large, bright room, consider using a translucent powder to smooth your complexion and eliminate any shine from your skin. If you tend to sweat heavily, you can rub some antiperspirant on your forehead and wash it off after your appearance. Spray a comb with hairspray and run it through your hair. It will smooth broken and flyaway ends. Make sure your hair never hides your face.

If you are offered the services of a professional makeup artist, by all means take advantage of their expertise. Men are sometimes reluctant to use makeup, but that's a mistake. Professional makeup will always improve your appearance under the lights and on camera. Women often assume that their everyday makeup will be sufficient. But the intense lighting of a television studio or big auditorium demands something more than ordinary cosmetics. Why risk looking washed out when expert professional help is available?

Try to check your appearance in a mirror one last time just before sitting down in front of the camera. Don't worry about looking vain. Your appearance is important. Why else would all this expensive equipment and high-paid staff be sitting in your office getting ready to take your picture? Comb and lightly spray your hair. Use a damp towel to wipe any oily sheen from your face and bring out color. But once you have dealt with your appearance off camera, forget about it and focus all your attention on what you want to say when the tape finally rolls.

Interview Mechanics

The reporter or producer is in charge of the interview, but the cameraperson ultimately decides who sits where and what type of lighting will be used. Unless you are convinced that the crew is doing something that will make you look less than your best, leave them alone to do their job. They are responsible for the overall visual quality of the story in which your interview will appear. Except in the most unusual cases, they will always try to use all their professional skill and experience to make both you and the story look as good as possible.

If the interview is taking place in your office, you may want to avoid sitting behind your desk unless you are deliberately trying to convey an image of command. If you appear too stiff and formal, you may come across as trying to hide behind your authority. If you adopt too relaxed a pose behind your desk, you may appear smug and superior. Viewers may respond negatively to your body language and not listen carefully to what you say. Unless you can avoid unconscious movement, try not to sit in a chair that swivels, tilts, or rocks. This will create problems for the cameraperson trying to keep you comfortably framed in the picture.

Many television interviews will be shot with bright artificial lights. Try to sit in front of the lights for a few minutes before the camera rolls. This helps your eyes adjust to the light level so you won't squint uncomfortably for the first part of the interview. Even today's small TV lights radiate a lot of heat. Sitting under the lights for a long time can get very uncomfortable. Pat your face free of perspiration before the camera is turned on, but never wipe perspiration away while the camera is rolling. If you start to really sweat during the interview, ask the reporter to turn off the camera for a moment so you can towel off.

Feel free to gesture naturally, especially if you are one of those people who feels comfortable talking with your hands. Spontaneous gestures are great for emphasis, illustration, and putting nervous energy to productive use. Trying deliberately not to gesture is an unnecessary distraction that will just make you more nervous and uncomfortable. Unless you suddenly jump up out of the chair, the cameraperson should have no trouble keeping you and your gestures safely in the picture.

After the questions and answers are over, the camera and lights may be moved around behind you. In order to provide more material for editing, these reverse cutaways are shot from the opposite angle, with you talking again for a few minutes and the reporter doing the same. Try to keep the same position you had during the interview, moving as little as possible. Excess movement makes these important cutaway shots difficult to use in editing. In rare instances, the reporter may repeat his questions as the reverse shots are being recorded. This allows the editor to smoothly integrate both the questions and the answers into the final product, making it look like the interview was shot with multiple cameras. Unfortunately, this technique also makes it easy for the reporter to revise his questions after you have already recorded your answers. Because it can so easily be abused in this way, some news organizations now forbid the practice as a matter of policy. These days, however, it is far more likely that the interview will be shot with two cameras in the first place, or if only one camera is used, that only your answers will appear in the final story.

Microphones

During the interview you will probably have a small microphone clipped to your lapel, tie, or dress. Don't try to speak down into the microphone. Just talk naturally with the reporter. Modern microphones are very sensitive, so even after the microphone is removed, assume you are still being recorded. And whatever you say probably will be picked up by the reporter's microphone as well.

If the reporter is using a hand-held microphone, never touch it. Even if the reporter's actions seem rude or provocative, never try to grab the microphone or push it away. The wrestling match will only make you look bad on the screen.

Just before the interview begins, the crew will ask you for a voice check. They aren't testing the microphone. That's already been done. They are just setting the recording level for your particular voice. Don't tap the microphone or blow into it. This may damage the equipment. Just say something in your normal conversational voice, perhaps your name and how to spell it, or count from one to ten and back again. Some people have very soft voices. Some range across dynamic levels, making it harder to establish accurate sound levels. If the crew asks for another microphone check, don't change your speech pattern. You aren't doing anything wrong. Just repeat what you said the first time, and don't alter your tone or volume unless you are specifically asked to do so. Never feel constrained to talk in a dull monotone just because the voice levels have been set. The sound system can handle a wide range of volume. During the interview the camera or sound person will be listening through an earphone and watching a meter in order to make sure that the sound is being recorded properly. If necessary, the level can be adjusted. Once the initial voice check is over, just forget about the sound and concentrate on the interview.

During the interview be careful not to fiddle with the microphone or its wires. This is a natural tendency, but you need to resist it. Microphones are very sensitive. If you must fiddle with something, make it a nice, quiet pencil, not a clicking ballpoint pen. Once the interview is underway, it is best to ignore the equipment entirely. Just talk to the reporter one-on-one, focusing solely on what you want to say.

The microphone is generally turned on during the entire setup process, so always assume that if there is a microphone in the room, it is live and recording every word you say. From the time the crew arrives until they are safely out the door, never say anything you wouldn't want to hear played back on the air. Once, during the taping of cutaways after an interview, a politician remarked casually to the reporter that the people in his district were so dumb they couldn't even spell the subject under discussion, let alone understand it. His candid comments were recorded perfectly of course, and not surprisingly, they quickly became the whole story. The unfortunate politician's constituents were fascinated to learn of his true feelings about them.

Relax

A bit of nervous energy keeps you sharp and alert. Almost everyone gets butterflies before an interview. The trick is to keep those butterflies flying in a controlled formation. Before the interview take a few deep breaths. The fresh oxygen will help relax you and your vocal chords. Sit comfortably, but don't slouch. Lean slightly forward in your chair. This body language sends a message of seriousness, concern, and engagement. Leaning back or slouching down in your chair sends a powerful visual message that you are uninterested, unconcerned, even a bit arrogant.

If you are seated behind a desk or table, put your hands on top with your forearms resting on the edge. When no desk or table is in front of you, keep your elbows on the chair arms in an open, nondefensive posture, or keep your hands together on one leg, between your hip and knee. Put your feet flat on the floor about two feet in front of the chair. Cross your legs at the knee if you wish, but don't bounce your upper leg. Let your hands rest in your lap, but don't clench them together. Turn them sideways or slightly upwards so you are always able to gesture naturally and comfortably if you feel like it.

Never nod "yes" while the reporter is asking a question. In casual conversation, many people are in the habit of nodding politely to indicate that they are listening and paying attention, even if they completely disagree with what's being said. But if you do this on television, your unconscious and otherwise benign gesture may leave the audience with the false impression that you are agreeing with something negative the reporter is saying or implying. Maintain a neutral expression while the question is being asked. Smiling or frowning may send the wrong signals at the wrong time. Save your expressions and gestures for the answers themselves, when they can help you make your point.

Ignore the camera. Always maintain firm eye contact with the interviewer. If sustained eye contact becomes uncomfortable or if the reporter looks down at his notes, focus instead on his ear, nose, or forehead. On-camera it will look just like you are making continuous eye contact. Never let your gaze drift off to the crew, cameras, monitors, ceiling, floor, or anything else that may be going elsewhere in the room.

Voice

Your voice makes an indelible impression in just the first few sentences you speak. Always try to achieve a confident, full-toned sound with enough melody and vocal variety to keep the audience comfortable and interested in what you are saying. Exercise your voice before the interview. Just as athletes warm up before a game, you can limber up your vocal cords, throat, jaws, tongue, lips, and the multitude of tiny muscles that are used in speech. Take several long, deep breaths before you speak. Feel that you are pulling in air all the way down to your toes. If you are prone to coughs or a scratchy throat, keep some cough drops in your pocket, but use them only before, never during, the interview.

Never drink anything too hot or too cold before or during the interview. It will constrict the back of your throat and could either numb or scorch your tongue, making it difficult to enunciate clearly. Don't drink alcoholic beverages or caffeine. Don't drink anything with bubbles. The best beverage for lubricating your voice under interview pressure is room temperature or slightly warmer water flavored with a bit of lemon juice. Never drink milk or eat cheese or chocolate before an interview. They can form mucous in the back of your throat and make you prone to distracting throat clearing.

Radio Talk Shows

Talk radio is an increasingly popular format that offers enormous strategic communications opportunities, as long as you understand what it is really all about and follow a few simple rules of the road. Talk radio is more about entertainment than information. Talk radio thrives on controversy. Except for a few noncommercial exceptions here and there, talk radio shows are usually looking harder for heat than they are for light. Except on the dullest and least popular talk shows, never expect to encounter a thoughtful exploration of complex issues. That's not the point of the format. Talk radio may promote the fact that it gives ordinary listeners a unique opportunity to participate and be heard, but successful talk radio programmers understand that the callers they put on the air are really no different than the records a music station chooses to play. Successful talk radio programmers try to choose their callers just as carefully, but perhaps not in exactly the way you might imagine.

For example, talk show callers are rarely selected to go on the air on a first come, first served basis. Of the tiny percentage of listeners who even try to call a popular talk show, an even tinier percentage will ever get on the air. Nor do the producers make any serious attempt to balance the flow of calls between the two sides of an issue. Callers are chosen instead for their entertainment value, their articulateness and intelligibility, the length of time they might be expected to talk, and their demographic characteristics. Talk show producers have even been known to prepare especially promising callers off the air by suggesting how they might frame their questions and comments for maximum impact and entertainment value.

When I was running the NBC TalkNet national radio network, we had the luxury of a nationwide audience listening on hundreds of local affiliates. We had an almost unlimited number of incoming calls to choose from. Our producers spent most of their time working with the very small number of callers they intended to put on the air. Those that didn't fit the format for some reason were quickly cut off or left on perpetual hold. I got my share of complaints from disappointed callers who felt that as loyal listeners they had a right to go on the air. But our job was not to please the callers, it was to make the programs as entertaining as possible for the listeners.

Caller demographics are particularly important to talk radio programmers. A talk radio program tends to attract listeners who roughly match the demographics of the callers it puts on the air.

For example, if a station puts a lot of elderly people on the air, elderly listeners will naturally feel more comfortable calling in to join the conversation. Elderly listeners will feel comfortable hearing callers who sound like themselves, and slowly but surely the station's audience will begin to skew older. Younger people will stop calling and, more important, they will stop listening. Nobody expects a country music station to play Mozart. Why would a talk station seeking to attract eighteen-to-twenty-four-year-old male listeners put a lot of elderly female callers on the air?

Talk show guests, on the other hand, are often carefully chosen to reflect both sides of a controversial issue, not in the interest of fairness and balance, but because lighting a fire under two articulate guests with deeply held and diametrically opposed points of view is a very good way to make an otherwise dull topic entertaining for ordinary listeners. But don't expect the host or the callers to be similarly fair and balanced. A talk show host has to be interesting and entertaining every hour of every show. In order to keep the rhetorical ball bouncing and the listening audience paying attention, the host may well take an outrageous or unexpected position just to generate equally outrageous and entertaining reactions from callers and guests. What the host really thinks about an issue is irrelevant. Talk show programming is about entertainment not enlightenment.

Keeping the show interesting and entertaining may be the talk show host's top priority, but your job as a guest is still to make your point to the listening audience. So, even in the heat of the moment during a particularly lively talk show, don't lose track of your planned responses, bridges, and key message. An hour of noisy debate with host, callers, and other guests can offer you a lot of opportunities to bridge back to your message and deliver it to a very attentive (if not always sympathetic) audience. Be prepared to take full advantage.

Interview Checklist

Before sitting down for any news media of interview, take time to review the following checklist:

- Find out before the interview as much as you can about what subjects will be covered, who else is being interviewed for the story, and the context in which the interview will be used.

- Learn as much as you possibly can about the news organization and the reporter with whom you will be dealing. Get the name of the reporter or producer who will be asking the questions, but never try to tell the news organization which reporter you prefer. Ask which topics the interviewer wants to cover, but never demand specific questions in advance.

- Know your strategic objective. The reporter's objective is to get a good story, to get you to "commit news." What's *your* objective? What do *you* hope to achieve in this interview?

- Anticipate likely areas of questioning. What issues is the reporter most likely to pursue given the overall context of the story as you understand it?

- Understand your audience. Who do you want to reach with your message and why? What do you want them to remember? Your audience is never the reporter. The interview is just a means to an end, a way for you to get your message to your real audience.

- Know what you *don't* want to say. You can't keep a reporter from asking difficult questions, but you can and should plan ahead for how you will handle them. And remember, there are some questions that you simply can't address (personnel matters, litigation).

Plan in advance how you will say so and how you will bridge to what you can talk about, your key message.

- Remember the point you came to make. Prepare your responses and, above all, your key message, and keep them firmly in mind during the interview. Imagine ahead of time how you would like to see the headline written or the sound bite selected. How do you want to be quoted? Does your message match your strategic objective?

- During the interview make sure to bridge to your key message as early and often as possible. Never fail to answer the reporter's question (if you can), but then immediately add a bridge, such as "but what's really most important here is . . ." and then deliver your key message

- Caution the news organization that you may not be the right person to interview if there are topics they want to ask about that you are unable to discuss due to lack of knowledge, litigation, trade secrets, etc. But never insist that they promise not to ask about certain subjects.

- Ask how long the interview will run and what the format will be, but never demand that your remarks be used without editing.

- Ask who else is being interviewed for the story, but never try to insist that the reporter not interview an adversary.

- Organize your information and practice your responses and messages, but don't just memorize canned answers.

- Practice answering the toughest questions you can think of and revise your approach as needed, but don't rehearse so much that you lose your spontaneity.

• Be brief. Refine your key message and responses to a few memorable lines. If you don't edit your message, the reporter will, and probably not the way you would prefer. Remember the message pyramid. Make your points and then back them up with facts, but never bury your main point in a mass of unnecessary detail.

• Don't ever say anything you wouldn't want quoted, no matter how hard the reporter may try to get you to do so. Assume that everything you say will be on the record.

• Beware of hypothetical ("what if?") questions. Stick to what you know. Never speculate just to please the reporter with a quick answer.

• Tell the truth no matter what. Don't be afraid to say you don't know. Anything you say, no matter how casually, that turns out to be wrong can quickly destroy your credibility. If you don't know the answer to a question, don't guess. Just offer to get the information for the reporter after the interview.

• Maintain eye contact. Always talk to the reporter, never the camera.

• Make your key message memorable by using stories, analogies, and examples. Most of us remember stories about real people longer than we do abstract discussions of even the most important issues.

• Avoid jargon. Speak in terms that real people can understand. Avoid complicated statistics and obscure acronyms.

• Never dismiss a question with "no comment." Be prepared to explain why you cannot talk about a subject.

- If you make a mistake, ask for an opportunity to correct it, but never demand that the reporter not use a botched answer. Never try to insist that something you said earlier be taken off the record.

- Remember that anything you say after the formal interview session is still on the record. Never assume that the microphones or camera have been turned off until they or you are out of the building.

- Always ask the reporter to call you if they have any further questions about something you have said, but never demand that a reporter show you a copy of the story prior to publication or broadcast.

- If you feel the story that is ultimately published or broadcast is inaccurate, call the reporter to politely point out what you think was wrong. Never call a reporter's supervisor to complain without first speaking with the reporter himself.

- Be yourself. In the end *you* will personify your message. If the audience responds positively to you personally, they will be much more likely to remember and respond positively to the point you are trying to make.

8 /

When the Going
Gets Rough

Communicating in a Crisis

A crisis can be defined as a bad situation that is rapidly getting worse. Between hostile media, angry neighbors, and a skeptical public, hard-won reputations are on the line, even as it gets more and more difficult for you to maintain control. Effective crisis management involves a lot more than communication of course, but developing and delivering messages that will reach and influence key audiences is an essential element of any effective crisis response. Putting out the fire is important, but explaining how the fire got started in the first place and helping people understand what you are doing to deal with it can make an enormous difference in their reactions. Effective communication can go a long way toward positioning you and your organization positively, even in a very bad situation. Indeed, most people are far more likely to judge an organization and its senior leaders on how well they are able to respond to a difficult situation than they are on what the organization may have done, or failed to do, that caused the problem in the first place.

Internal Communication

Obviously, the best way to manage any potential crisis situation is to keep it from becoming a full-fledged crisis in the first place. The first goal of crisis management, therefore, is always prevention. Effective communication, especially good *internal* communication, plays a critical role. Effective internal communication can help an organization identify and deal with potential crisis situations while there is still time to take preventive action before they get out of hand. Some years ago, when a Mitsubishi automobile plant in Illinois was slapped with a multi-million-dollar sexual harassment lawsuit it came as a shock to the general public, but it should not have been a surprise to anyone familiar with what had been going on at the plant. Almost as soon as the story broke it became abundantly clear that female plant workers had been complaining for years about various forms of sexual harassment. It was common knowledge throughout the plant, but plant managers either never heard the message or chose to ignore it. If there had been better internal communication, if the plant managers had been listening to their workers and paying proper attention, they almost certainly would have been able to address the sexual harassment problem as soon as it first appeared, and well before it rose to the level of an accident looking for a place to happen. Paying closer attention to what was happening all around the plant, and doing something about it, would have helped plant managers avoid a costly lawsuit and a lot of bad publicity. No matter how well an organization is able to identify potential problems and solve them before they escalate, however, it is always wise to prepare for the worst situations you can imagine. The best way to prepare efficiently for worst-case scenarios is to take a broad systems approach to crisis management.

Systems Approach

There are three distinct phases in the systems approach to crisis management: preparation, response, and recovery. *Preparation* involves putting together a solid crisis plan, training people to use it, validating the plan with realistic drills and exercises, and continuously updating and fine-tuning it in response to new information and changing circumstances. *Response* involves efficiently activating and implementing the plan as soon as a problem occurs. *Recovery* is about getting back to normal as quickly as possible when the acute phase of a crisis has passed, taking time to carefully review what happened, how well the organization responded, and revising crisis plans accordingly so that they will work better the next time. Lessons learned in the recovery stage will help prevent future situations from escalating to the crisis stage and prepare the organization to deal with any unexpected problems that may occur.

Before looking in more detail at the overall process of crisis management and prevention and the specific role of communication in crisis planning and response, it is important first to ask a very simple question: What makes a crisis a crisis in the first place? Not every unexpected emergency or lingering problem automatically explodes into a full-blown crisis. Indeed, only a small percentage ever do. That's due in part to pure luck, but it also speaks to the importance of good planning, quick response, and careful crisis assessment. A key part of any comprehensive crisis plan is an orderly system by which members of the senior crisis management team can efficiently assess a potential crisis situation and determine the appropriate level of internal and external response. Undertaking a full scale crisis response to every unexpected situation is a waste of time and resources and will probably do nothing but make matters worse. A bad day at the office is not necessarily a crisis, and the first responsibility of a well-prepared crisis management team is to clearly understand the difference.

Some years ago, one of my partners and I were summoned halfway around the world to help a major client deal with what they were convinced was a very serious crisis situation. Our client, a regional division of a large multinational corporation, was sure that a competitor was "dumping" a commodity product on the local market, selling at well below their cost in order to capture an unfair market share. As soon as we arrived at the client's office we sat down with the top managers to examine the situation and go through an orderly process of crisis assessment.

The client's crisis team was convinced that their competitor was getting away with dumping because of its close connections with the country's corrupt government officials. Our client was seriously considering a bold strategy that would have had them leverage their own government connections in order to counter those of their competitor. The government of the country in question was undeniably corrupt, but on closer examination, there was no credible evidence that government corruption was playing a significant role in this situation. And it should go without saying that trying to counter a competitor's alleged corruption by engaging in similar corrupt behavior yourself is a highly questionable and dangerous strategy. It was not something my partner and I felt comfortable even discussing.

Before engaging the team in any deep ethical or philosophical discussions, however, our first move was to pull them back to the fundamentals. We helped the crisis team work through the essential first step in any crisis response: a careful, unemotional analysis of what was really going on, what it meant, and where it might possibly lead. It didn't take very long for everyone involved in the discussion to realize that this situation really wasn't a crisis at all, and it certainly didn't need to become one. It was a difficult business problem, but despite the obvious financial implications, that was all it was. In fact, it was clear, to us at least, that the clever competitor was simply pursuing a strategy not much different from the one on which our client's business was also based. They were buying commodities in the lowest-priced markets they could find around the world and then selling them in markets where they would command the highest prices. This was hardly a business model that required anyone to start bribing government officials.

Had our client jumped reflexively into crisis mode they would likely have made their problem much worse. They might even have created a crisis where none existed. We helped them avoid that pitfall by enforcing an orderly process of issue identification. What's really going on? What does it really mean? What is the worst-case outcome? What are the options available to deal with it, and what are the potential implications, good and bad, of each of those response options? Most of our clients over the years have been perfectly capable of coming up with answers for themselves, but they almost always needed an objective outsider to ask the right questions.

Defining a Crisis

Expanding on our definition of a crisis being a bad situation getting worse, let's look at it as something that happens unexpectedly and causes serious damage to the organization or interferes with its normal way of doing business.

This might include accidents such as fires, explosions, marine casualties, spills, product contamination, product failures, or transportation mishaps. A crisis can also be triggered by criminal activity, such as arson, bombings, extortion, hijackings, hostage situations, kidnapping, murder, and product tampering. Another obvious category includes natural disasters, such as earthquakes, floods, forest fires, hurricanes, landslides, snowstorms, tornadoes, and even volcanoes. Finally, there are marketplace and political problems, such as activist group protests, conflicts on the board of directors, sudden breakthroughs by competitors, criminal indictments of managers or employees, damaging rumors, government investigations, hostile takeovers, labor strife, restrictive regulation, lawsuits, and unfavorable media attention.

While such lists are a convenient way to begin the process of thinking broadly about all the different events that could possibly escalate into a full-blown crisis, each individual organization must assess very carefully which specific events would be the most likely to affect its particular operation and which of those would pose the greatest potential threat to its continuing operation or reputation. The dangers faced by a chemical plant or an oil refinery are obviously very different from those for which a university campus needs to be prepared.

Considering a crisis merely as an unpredictable and unpleasant event, however, still leaves an organization in a reactive mode. In fact, as the Mitsubishi example illustrates, most crises don't occur at random. Nor is all the damage they cause merely the immediate result of any one specific event. In fact, while the element of surprise and unpredictability would seem to be at the core of what most of us think of as a crisis, the vulnerabilities that can lead to a crisis situation are often highly predictable and usually preventable.

Simmering Problems

A broader and deeper definition of a crisis is a damaging situation triggered by a sudden event or a *simmering problem,* such as the sexual harassment situation at that automobile plant. Among other things, this definition draws a valuable distinction between the *objective* and *subjective* impacts of any serious crisis situation, a distinction that is absolutely critical to effective crisis communication.

Objective impacts are the most obvious: injury or loss of life, environmental damage, long-term health effects, and physical damage to property. Subjective impacts are more subtle, often reflecting long-term changes in public perception caused by a crisis event, and even more important, by an organization's response to it. These perceived problems include mismanagement, negligence, failure to warn, failure to deal effectively with sudden dangerous situations, and poor communications during an emergency response.

Objective impacts are usually easier to observe and measure than subjective impacts. It is a lot easier for most of us to see a burned-out building than it is to appreciate a subtle shift in public attitude. But subjective damage to an organization's reputation can be even more substantial and long-lasting. An organization may have a hard time understanding and accepting the subjective impact of an adverse event, especially when the objective impact does not by itself seem to justify the public's perception of the seriousness of the situation. For example, a fatal accident may attract a lot of negative attention for a short period of time and then fade from public view forever. That's the objective impact. But an environmental incident in which nobody was harmed but which nevertheless creates doubt and concern in the community may persist as a high-profile issue for months or even years. That's the subjective impact. The most severe subjective impact is usually the result of a crisis situation in which others perceive that an organization has failed to do the right thing before, as well as during and after, the incident itself.

Systems Definition

This leads to still another definition of crisis, the *systems definition*. The systems definition takes into account the state of an organization's culture before, during, and after a sudden damaging event or as the result of a long-simmering problem. This way of looking at a crisis situation focuses on how an organization deals proactively with events, trends, and warning signals that could eventually lead to serious problems. This approach to crisis management pays particular attention to the preparation stage during which an organization has an opportunity to identify warning signs, assess its particular vulnerabilities, and consider the relative probability of any of these potential problems actually occurring. This in turn, allows the organization to focus its energy on preparing for potential crises based on a thoughtful assessment of both vulnerability and probability.

A realistic crisis assessment should be based on factors such as whether a situation could suddenly intensify, whether it might attract attention from the media or government regulators, whether it might jeopardize the organization's public image and reputation, how seriously and for how long it might interfere with normal operations, how seriously it might impact sales or revenue, whether it would have a negative effect on employee morale and productivity, whether it would effect market value, and whether it might lead to expensive lawsuits or troublesome new regulations.

While this approach to crisis management is preferable to a purely event-oriented view, there is still another way of thinking about potential crisis situations that is even more proactive. *Webster's Dictionary* defines *crisis* as: "A decisive moment . . . a crucial time . . . a turning point for better or worse." In other words, strange as it may seem, even a very serious crisis need not be an entirely negative experience for an organization. Indeed, despite the obvious short-term challenges, even a potentially very damaging crisis situation can offer an organization important long-term opportunities. Many companies have emerged from a serious crisis considerably stronger than they were before, not to mention being much better prepared for anything similar that might happen in the future. It all depends on how well the organization manages the situation and how well it is able to communicate with key audiences when the going gets rough.

The best-known example of how this works is Johnson & Johnson's now-famous response to the 1983 Tylenol tampering situation. When innocent people died after swallowing Tylenol capsules mysteriously laced with cyanide, most observers figured the popular pain reliever was history. But Johnson & Johnson CEO, James Burke, moved quickly to address the tragic situation by taking every last package of Tylenol off the shelves nationwide without regard to the potential cost. He then went on national television to make it clear that the company had no intention of selling the product again until it could be made safe from similar tampering. The public was relieved and grateful. The story shifted

quickly from the deadly threat of tainted Tylenol to a compassion-
ate and responsible company's heroic efforts to protect public
health and safety in the wake of criminal attack, what today would
be called terrorism.

Many companies faced with similar situations feel compelled
to defend themselves against charges that they were somehow
negligent, charges they consider to be unfounded and unfair.
They correctly observe that, far from being the perpetrator of a
crime, the company is itself a victim, and perhaps even the criminal's primary target. Unfortunately, however, even such a seem-
ingly reasonable response to irresponsible charges inevitably
comes across as uncomfortably defensive. It sends a message that
perhaps the company really does have something to be defensive
about after all. This, of course, is the exact opposite of what an
effective crisis response should try to accomplish. Above all, such
a defensive response appears to put the company's interests ahead
of those of its customers, the very people it needs to reach with its
message at a critical time.

Instead of responding to the crisis in terms of what mattered
most to the company, such as lost sales and potential legal liability, Johnson & Johnson focused first and foremost on the safety
concerns of its customers. What could easily have been a multi-
billion-dollar blow to Johnson & Johnson's bottom line quickly
turned into a golden opportunity to improve the product and
enhance the company's reputation. Johnson & Johnson took full
advantage of that huge communications opportunity, and Tylenol
soon returned to the shelves in tamper-proof packaging. It quickly
recaptured its previous market share and then some. On the
strength of that one high-profile incident, Johnson & Johnson
has been recognized ever since as the gold standard for effective
crisis response.

Problems and Solutions

Reporters are always looking for bad news, for someone to blame. That's what makes for a good story. But the general public is often a lot more interested in what is being done to solve a serious problem than they are in finding out who caused it. Look at what happened when Dell faced a potentially devastating situation after news reports began to appear describing how some of their notebook computer batteries were spontaneously overheating and catching fire. Nobody who carries a notebook computer, especially on airplanes, could feel particularly comfortable knowing that it might suddenly explode, but according to stories spreading across the Internet and mainstream media, millions of Dell notebooks were apparently at serious risk of doing just that. Moreover, the track record of most computer companies at managing consumer problems of this magnitude is not great, and Dell itself was already experiencing well-publicized problems with customer service.

In fact, the exploding laptop batteries weren't even made by Dell. They were supplied by Sony and could be found in several other brands of computers as well. Of all the millions of similar batteries in use, only a tiny percentage had ever caught fire, and none had done any serious damage, except to the computer. But rather than fall prey to an understandable temptation to shift the blame, minimize the problem, or spin some other type of defensive response, Dell wisely decided to address the core issue: customer confidence. Anyone carrying a Dell notebook computer wanted to be reassured that it was not a ticking time bomb. If they did happen to own one of the defective batteries, they wanted to know what they could do to protect themselves. Even if a solid factual case could have been made that the batteries were not really a serious safety problem, that argument would have fallen on deaf ears once scare stories about exploding computers were out on the Internet. Hard as it may be for many engineers to accept, ordinary people faced with a potentially serious threat care very little about the actual facts, they just want to be reassured that they aren't going to be injured or killed. They aren't looking for trouble, but neither do they want their deepest fears dismissed by arrogant company experts telling them they have nothing to worry about.

Timing

Timing is important. Even the best crisis response can fail if it comes too late in the process. A good example was AOL's reaction to reports that personal information relating to more than a half million of its subscribers had mistakenly been posted on a public Web site. AOL had a solid reputation for its corporate commitment to personal privacy, and this particular security breach was not the result of any technical failure or a flawed corporate policy. It was simply a matter of bad judgment on the part of an AOL employee. Eventually, two midlevel employees were fired and the senior manager in charge of the unit resigned voluntarily. But none of this happened until the beleaguered company had already suffered several weeks of brutal attacks from suspicious bloggers and angry personal privacy activists.

To its credit, AOL was quick to follow the first two steps in the crisis communications process. The company promptly accepted responsibility for the problem and restated its long-standing commitment to online privacy. But the all-important action step was far too late in coming. Until it did, competitors and privacy advocates had a free hand to make AOL the poster child for a broad range of online privacy issues. Even the dramatic departure of the senior company official responsible for privacy policy turned out to be too little, too late, once the problem was allowed to spiral out of control. Especially in an environment of almost instantaneous news coverage and pervasive online commentary, speed is of the essence in crisis response and communication.

Crisis Assessment

Just as every emergency or unexpected event is not automatically a crisis, all crisis situations are not created equal. Of all the risks an organization might possibly face, some would undoubtedly cause serious damage, while others would cause very little. Some would cause more objective than subjective damage, and vice versa. Some events are very likely to happen, while others are only a very remote possibility. The first step in the organized analysis of vulnerabilities and probabilities is to consider as many worst-case scenarios as possible. For the process to work effectively you need to think broadly and creatively. Even if your organization already has an elaborate plan for handling product recalls, or chemical spills, or some other situation common in your particular industry, you should take a step back to consider all the other far less obvious situations that might seriously interfere with the way you routinely conduct your business.

Once you have assembled this master list of worst-case scenarios (and it could easily run to several dozen), carefully rate each one on a scale of 1 to 10, with 1 representing the least potential damage to the organization and 10 representing the greatest. For example, if your company operates a single plant, a fire that destroys that plant probably would put you out of business. That's a 10. But if you have a number of plants scattered across the country, a fire that puts any one of them out of commission would be troublesome, but probably not devastating. That's maybe a 3 or 4. If your plant receives vital raw materials in daily shipments and that just-in-time supply chain were somehow interrupted for a few days, the impact might be inconvenient and costly, but probably wouldn't bring your business to a permanent standstill. Give it a 2 or 3 on the vulnerability scale. For the time being, do *not* consider the likelihood that any particular scenario might actually happen. However unlikely it may seem that you would ever have to deal with a particular situation, confine yourself to evaluating only the seriousness of the damage you would suffer if it did.

When you have scored all your worst-case scenarios for relative vulnerability, you are ready to rate each as to the probability that it might actually happen. For example, if your plant is located on the bank of a river, floods are probably more likely than if the plant were located on high ground in a dry climate. If a particular event has actually occurred recently at your facility or one like it, logic suggests that there is a higher probability that something similar might occur again. The key to this process is to always score the probability and vulnerability of each scenario separately. How likely a particular situation is to occur should never influence your consideration of how serious it would be if it did. How serious it would be must never be allowed to influence your assessment of how likely it is to happen.

When scoring individual scenarios according to vulnerability and probability, it is often helpful to start right in the middle, with a score of 5, and then either move the score up or down as you look at the scenario more carefully and consider all its various aspects. If you start the process at either extreme you are more likely to skew the results in one direction or another and thereby make the final analysis far less useful overall. Starting in the middle of the scale makes it less likely that you will end up with most or all of your scenarios scoring 9s and 10s or 1s and 2s. A reasonable spread of scores across the full 10-point spectrum is far more realistic. It is also a very good idea to involve as many different functions in the organization as possible in the vulnerability and probability analysis. The concerns of the IT department are likely to be very different from those of the people in charge of the plant floor. The legal, safety, human resources, and sales departments are all likely to come up with their own lists of vulnerabilities and their own assessment of probabilities.

Finally, look at the individual probability and vulnerability scores you have assigned to each of the scenarios you have considered. Anything that scored 5 or higher for both probability and vulnerability is probably a serious threat that is worth examining more closely to make sure you are properly prepared to deal with it. Your next priority is not nearly as obvious, however. It is those scenarios that score low on the probability scale (not very likely to happen), but high on the vulnerability scale (likely to cause very serious problems if they did). Because they are so unlikely, scenarios in this category are easy to overlook or ignore. But that is a dangerous mistake. Worst case means just that, and a good crisis plan pays close attention to the worst that could possibly happen, even if it is very unlikely. Obviously, scenarios with both low probability and low vulnerability, while they can't be ignored altogether, fall far lower on the priority list.

Crisis Management

In order to properly manage a crisis an organization must have effective command, control, and communications systems. There must be clear lines of authority and clearly defined responsibilities and lines of communication. Hardware and software requirements must be anticipated and prepared for in advance. Training and practice are essential to keeping the crisis plan fine-tuned and the people who will be called upon to execute it fully prepared to do so at a moment's notice. If your organization already has a crisis management plan in place, take another look at it to make sure the following basic items are adequately covered:

- Preparation
- Training
- Early warning systems
- Notification mechanisms
- Quick decision-making capability
- Clear lines of authority
- Easy access to vital information
- Flexibility to adjust to changing conditions
- Rapid response capability

When preparing to deal with crisis situations, an organization must make sure that its chain of command is not so cumbersome that it would be difficult to approve quick action and timely public statements under pressure. If yours is a large organization, decision-making authority should be delegated down to managers in the field whenever possible. Those on the scene of a rapidly developing situation are in a much better position to know what's happening and how to handle it than anyone back at headquarters. Local executives already well known in the local community are likely to have far greater credibility with key constituencies than higher-ranking officials who have just flown in from out of town.

Preparation is crucial. Since every possible contingency cannot be predicted in advance, it is important to address those things which can be handled ahead of time (e.g., communications planning, logistics, personnel assignments, fact sheet preparation, hardware purchases, etc.) so that when the worst happens the crisis management team will be able to devote all its attention to the specific problem at hand. A crisis is a bad time to be playing catch-up.

Crisis Communication

Like any other aspect of crisis management and response, crisis communication is all about time. There is rarely enough time to do everything that needs to be done under the intense pressure that a crisis situation always creates. But there are some overall crisis communications goals that you should keep in mind no matter what the situation.

• **Reduce tension.** In an emergency, the corporate spokesperson must take care to avoid inadvertently creating panic either internally or externally. The spokesperson must be calm and authoritative.

• **Demonstrate problem solving.** Your spokesperson should emphasize what is being done to cope with the problem at hand. Knowing what is being done to deal with a crisis situation is usually more important to most members of the public than knowing who might have been responsible for creating the bad situation in the first place. The public is less interested in assigning blame than in being reassured that things are getting back to normal.

- **Tell the public what's happening.** While this suggestion may seem rather obvious, the spokesperson may not always know everything that is going on at every level during a crisis response. Gathering accurate information is essential, but getting as much of that information out to the public and the media as quickly as possible is even more important. If you insist on waiting until you know everything before allowing your spokesperson to speak to the public and meet the media, you will never be able to communicate effectively, and the audiences you need to reach will probably conclude that you have something to hide or, even worse, that you just don't know what you're doing.

- **Tell people what they can do to help.** Those affected by a crisis are usually willing to help deal with it. If there is anything they can do to help, make sure to let them know. In some situations (a major chemical spill, for example) the best advice is probably to stay inside with the windows closed. But if there is any way to provide a safe outlet for the public's natural urge to help themselves and their families by participating in the crisis response, make sure to offer it. Otherwise some people may choose to react to the situation by spreading rumors, joining destructive protests, or even engaging in outright obstruction.

- **Tell the truth.** The facts are fundamental. Your organization's hard-won credibility is at stake. During the nuclear power plant emergency at Three Mile Island, for example, the owners of the plant failed to respond accurately to legitimate and obvious media inquiries at the start of the incident. The entire nuclear power industry has been paying the price for that devastating loss of credibility ever since.

As with all communications situations, to be effective during a crisis your messages must always be responsive to the emotional concerns of the audience. People want to know what's going on, of course, but they are far more interested in what it means to them and those they care about. The media are an important way to reach an audience, but they are only a means to an end, not an end in themselves. The media themselves are never your target audience. Their readers, listeners, and viewers are.

Some general guidelines for dealing effectively with the news media during a crisis:

- Always speak with one voice and avoid contradictory comments.
- Never make unauthorized or unrealistic promises.
- Always show commitment and empathy.
- Always emphasize what is being done to solve the problem.
- Neutralize negative rumors as quickly as possible.
- Always provide timely updates to the media, the public, and those in your own organization.

Especially in a crisis situation, stonewalling does not work. The more you try to keep something secret, the more aggressively reporters and activists will work to get at the truth. If you are ever suspected of deliberately lying or trying to hide something significant, the media and the public will naturally be more inclined to believe whatever negative rumors they hear about you. Any effort to derail a media investigation will only increase the media's interest. The slower the flow of information to the media and the public, the longer your recovery from the crisis is likely to take.

Once a decision is made to communicate via the news media,

it is absolutely essential that the spokesperson be thoroughly prepared. Fortunately, there is a simple checklist for efficient spokesperson preparation, similar to the interview checklist in the previous chapter:

- Obtain and organize the facts.
- Identify the key audiences.
- Anticipate questions and areas of concern.
- Decide specifically what you want to say in response.
- Decide what you must avoid saying.
- Have a story to tell and a point to make.

In the midst of a confusing and rapidly changing crisis situation, reporters are always looking for hard facts. They want truthful, quick, concise answers to their specific questions. They want information boiled down to the essentials, and they want you to give them that information in simple, comprehensible terms. Even if they already know the key facts, reporters will still want good quotes. They will still need you to put things on the record in terms they can use. And reporters always appreciate guidance on the theme of the story. This is your opportunity to help the reporter tell the story as you would like it told. If a fire is still burning out of control, the basic story line is obvious. But when the flames have gone out, the way you have framed the story may well determine whether your organization and its crisis response efforts are presented to the public in a positive or a negative light.

Some pitfalls to avoid when trying to communicate in a crisis situation:

- Lying (never misrepresent the facts).
- Speculating (hypothetical questions are dangerous).

- Blaming (anyone).
- Guessing (if you don't know, just say so).
- Naming victims (unless families have been notified).
- Dwelling on negative allegations (stress positive solutions instead).
- Losing your cool (ever).
- Saying "no comment" (always give a good reason for not answering a question).
- Attempting to go "off the record" (there is no such thing in the real world).
- Improvising (stick to your strategic message).
- Arguing with reporters (they always have the last word).
- Cracking jokes (they can easily backfire).
- Delaying (always respect the reporter's deadline).

Avoiding hypothetical questions can be very difficult for those who are trained and experienced at developing contingency plans and preparing responses to "what if?" scenarios. But whenever a "what if?" question is asked, try to bring the focus back to what is actually happening. At Three Mile Island, public fears escalated sharply when government spokespeople carelessly speculated about scary "what ifs?" instead of sticking to what was known to be happening at the site.

Focus, Target, Calibrate

To be effective, the messages you deliver must be carefully calibrated to fit the situation at hand. Just because you *can* say something doesn't necessarily mean you should. In addition to being mindful of tone and style, you must make sure that your answers don't inadvertently undermine or overwhelm the story you want to tell or make an already bad situation even worse. Avoid the temptation to raise extraneous or potentially troublesome issues that could risk turning a routine story into a front-page headline or an already difficult story into a full-blown disaster.

Crisis communications experts love to tell the story, perhaps apocryphal, about a chemical plant manager who came down to the gate to give interviews to the local media after a potentially disastrous fire was successfully extinguished with no deaths, injuries, or serious damage. Everything was going fine until one of the reporters inquired about a very large tank that stood near the plant gate. The tank had not been involved in the fire, but the reporter was curious about what was in it. The plant manager responded with the name of an unfamiliar and nearly unpronounceable chemical. The curious reporter followed up by asking what would have happened if the fire had somehow spread to that tank. "It would have been like Hiroshima," the plant manager quickly and carelessly responded.

Oops. Instead of the positive story line about how well his plant had managed to deal effectively with a dangerous situation, the story would now be all about how a major catastrophe had been narrowly averted. The theme of the story would be the huge danger the plant still posed to the health and safety of anyone living nearby. All because the plant manager fell prey to the temptation to speculate about what *might* have happened instead of focusing on what actually *did* happen and sticking to the positive message about his plant's effective firefighting capabilities. That unhappy plant manager learned the hard way how important it is to *focus* on your audience (workers and neighbors), *target* your message to that specific audience (what's being done to solve the problem and keep everyone safe), and above all, *calibrate* your responses so that you don't inadvertently make a good story bad or a bad story worse.

Similarly, offering inaccurate statistics, even inadvertently, will badly damage your credibility. Avoid guesses and lowball figures. They may have to be increased later. Keep things as simple as possible. Avoid complicated numbers that will only confuse people. If the numbers you have are preliminary, stress that they are only preliminary. Whenever possible, coordinate the release of numbers to the media with their release to government agencies. That will help keep you from being upstaged by government spokespeople and made to look like you are holding something back from the public. Reporters will eventually get their hands on just about any document you release to any government agency anyway, so never refuse to turn over those documents to the media. If you do, it will appear that you have something to hide. And never try to cover up public documents that contain negative information.

Avoid overly technical terminology and industry jargon. Even though you may just be trying to be as precise as possible, technical terms can be misleading to the uninitiated and might send the unintended message that you are deliberately trying to confuse the audience. Avoid words and phrases that promise too much or sound too good to be true (even if they are). Beware of unnecessary superlatives, such as: "We'll clean up every drop we spilled." That's a promise you could never keep and don't want to be on record as ever having made. Avoid casual comments. They can easily be misinterpreted. Stick firmly to your strategic message no matter what.

Carelessly quoting third-party endorsements can easily backfire. You have no control over anyone outside your organization, and a third party you are counting on for support in a crisis might suddenly pull back when the heat is on. It is much safer, as well as more credible, to encourage inquisitive reporters to contact friendly third parties on their own, so those third parties can speak for themselves.

Good communication in crisis situations reflects careful planning and sound corporate decision making. It is important for senior management to recognize right from the start that any failure to communicate effectively will send a strong negative signal to the public, one that will always reflect badly on the company. When assessing the state of your organization's overall crisis communications preparedness try going through this simple precrisis checklist:

- Are your standby statements and fact sheets up-to-date and accessible after hours?
- Are your spokespeople and backups designated?
- Are all your spokespeople well trained to deal with the media and the public under the pressure of a crisis situation?
- Are your spokespeople fully authorized to answer questions and knowledgeable enough to do so effectively?
- Is there sufficient phone, radio, and other communication gear standing by and easily available to crisis team members?
- Are enough computers, printers, copiers, fax machines, Internet connections, and other vital communications resources available to the crisis management team and your spokespeople?
- Do you have a system in place for answering outside calls after hours?
- Is a member of the crisis team always on duty after hours?
- Are they equipped with a mobile phone or portable e-mail device?
- Do you have an effective and well-tested management notification system in place?
- Are your lists of contacts (media, outside experts, community leaders, etc.) up to date?

- Do you have twenty-four-hour access to outside crisis communications counsel and support?

Effective crisis communication demands consistency and focus. A principal spokesperson and an alternate should be designated in advance as part of your overall crisis plan. When responding to a crisis situation, your organization should be prepared to speak with only one voice and consistently deliver the same key messages. For example, many crisis communications plans overlook or ignore the need to instruct all staff, and especially those likely to be answering outside phone calls, that they should refer all questions and inquiries about the crisis situation only to the company's designated spokespeople. As far as the media and other outsiders are concerned, whoever answers the phone first is an authorized company spokesperson, and whatever that person says will be taken as an official company statement.

Offering conflicting messages from different spokespeople or different parts of the company will quickly destroy your organization's overall credibility. At Three Mile Island, a lot of unnecessarily negative news coverage and even a bit of panic resulted when conflicting messages were given to the media by personnel at the site and others back in Washington. When that happens, and it happens all too often in serious crisis situations, both the media and the public will assume that little or nothing they are being told by anyone is really the truth, and all your communications efforts will have been a waste of time.

Characteristics of the ideal crisis spokesperson include:

- Composure and tact.
- Common sense.
- Alertness and stamina.

- Seniority in the organization.
- Knowledge and credibility.
- Ability to translate technical information into layman's terms.

Court of Public Opinion

High-profile litigation is one crisis situation where a strategic approach to communication can make an enormous difference to the outcome. We all live and work in an increasingly litigious environment. If your company makes anything or does anything that could possibly be perceived as ever being harmful to someone else, the odds are that you eventually will be sued. Or you may find yourself on the other side, as the plaintiff in a lawsuit that attracts a lot of public and media attention. Either way, the legal strategy itself will be the responsibility of the lawyers. But with your reputation and perhaps the value of your brand on the line, you will need more than just your legal team involved right from the start.

Inside the courtroom the rules of procedure and evidence are very clear. They are designed to enforce fairness and establish a level playing field. In the world outside the courthouse, however, entirely different rules apply. Inside the courtroom, in theory at least, facts matter above all. Outside what matters most are perceptions. As you would expect, lawyers trying a case in court concern themselves with what is legally significant, not necessarily what is most important to the general public. Arguments and evidence carefully assembled to persuade jurors in the controlled environment of a courtroom are often ineffective, and may even be counterproductive, with other important audiences such as customers and investors. And what good does it do to win your case in court if the public fallout has already destroyed your company? In the wake of the Enron collapse the Arthur Andersen accounting firm was quickly put out of business by a federal indictment. Thousands of people lost their jobs. Andersen was eventually exonerated in court, but by that time it no longer mattered. The company had been destroyed. Ignoring the realities of the court of public opinion is like stepping in front of a speeding car in the certain knowledge that you have the legal right of way. Even if you turn out to be right, proving the point will probably cost you your life.

As with any comprehensive crisis communications effort, preparation is the key to a successful litigation communication plan. Whether you are the defendant or the plaintiff, you must make sure that communication is part of your overall litigation strategy right from the start. And even before there is actual litigation, it pays to keep a close eye on emerging trends. After WorldCom, Enron, and other major business scandals, corporate governance became the flavor of the month. Meeting the politically driven requirements of new federal regulations such as those created by the 2002 Sarbanes-Oxley Act was only the beginning. These days companies with fine reputations and no regulatory compliance issues whatever can easily find themselves targets of corporate governance interest groups, activists, and plaintiff's lawyers eager to hold your corporate reputations for ransom.

This sort of scrutiny is often unfair, of course, and in the long run you may not be in any real legal jeopardy. But like the fellow standing in the middle of the street demanding the right of way, that won't matter much when demonstrators appear at your plant, plaintiff's lawyers come calling, and regulators hit you with subpoenas. Better to practice good issues management, recognize the risks, and prepare in advance to deal with them, just as you would prepare for fires, floods, or any other potential crisis situation. Never let yourself be surprised by a sudden extortion demand from a plaintiff's lawyer or activist group. Aggressively communicating concern and commitment, doing so as early as possible, and demonstrating tangible action in support of that corporate commitment are essential steps in the initial phase of litigation communication, just as they are in the acute stage of crisis communication generally.

A very important first step in any well-designed litigation communications strategy is a wide ranging vulnerability assessment. Legal risks are no different than any of the other vulnerabilities you face, and you should treat them the same way. Take the broadest possible view and consider the worst-case scenarios. Think carefully about how bad it would be if nothing goes your way and you will be better prepared for whatever happens. Above all, when considering the vulnerabilities created by a particular litigation situation, you will want to assess carefully how much attention the case is likely to attract and who is likely to be paying attention.

We once handled the communications side of a very sizeable product liability class action brought against a well-known manufacturing company. Among the things that made the case interesting was the fact that the product involved was not something for which the company was particularly well known. It was essentially a side business. That turned out to be very significant when we began to analyze the audience and its concerns. On the one hand, the risk that publicity surrounding litigation involving even a minor product might spill over and harm our client's overall reputation was obvious. Indeed, like all good plaintiff's lawyers, the other side in this case was not a bit shy about promoting their allegations in the media, in part at least because this tactic was proving very successful at attracting new plaintiffs to the case, plaintiffs who had no idea that there might even be a problem with the product until they read about it in newspaper stories planted by the plaintiff's lawyers.

But our client had a potentially powerful card to play as well. Opinion polls that we conducted in the state where most of the complaints originated found that our client had a sterling reputation. Indeed, when asked about the other side's messages, an overwhelming majority of those we surveyed expressed surprise that such a well-known and well-respected company could possibly be responsible for the unexpected product failures the plaintiffs were alleging. Moreover, we found, not surprisingly, that interest in this particular litigation was limited to a very small number of people, essentially those who had reason to believe that they might already have the allegedly defective product in their homes. With that in mind, our communications strategy was carefully calibrated to target only that specific audience without attracting unwanted attention among the much larger number of people who thought well of our client and didn't have a personal interest in the problem. Above all, we tried to tell a positive story that would counteract the other side's scare tactics and reassure those who had the product in their homes that they really had nothing to worry about as long as it had been properly installed and maintained. A key element of our campaign was to educate potential plaintiffs about proper maintenance procedures that would prevent problems with the product from happening in the first place. Inside the courtroom, this case was all about helping jurors understand and appreciate complicated engineering. Outside the courtroom it was all about dealing with the irrational fears of a very different audience.

Just as the best crisis is one that never happens in the first place, the best outcome in most litigation communications situations is lack of interest on the part of the media and the general public. Another potentially high-profile case we handled involved a firm well known in its own industry, but completely unknown outside it. The company faced a federal criminal indictment for fraudulent billing practices involving government contracts. The numbers were potentially huge, and the risk that the company would be barred from future government contracts was significant. Indeed, it might well have put the company out of business. While the legal defense team got to work negotiating a plea bargain, we analyzed the potential fallout. The target audience was very small, essentially the company's current and potential clients and, of course, its own employees. Initial coverage of the case was limited to a few trade publications that followed the industry closely. Because our client was all but unknown outside its own business there was essentially no general media interest. One of our most important strategic objectives was to keep it that way.

The plea-bargain discussion dragged on for the better part of four years, but right from the start we advised our client to be as forthcoming as possible with their employees and clients. The CEO personally reached out to key clients to explain the situation and what the company was doing to deal with it. Because of the delicate and complicated legal maneuvers that were going on, this was not always as simple as it might seem. There were aspects of the case that the lawyers refused to allow us to discuss, even internally. But even with that limitation, a sincere expression of concern and a demonstrated commitment to positive remedial action were crucial to maintaining customer trust and employee loyalty. Clients were understandably concerned that they might be doing business with a criminal organization. Employees were concerned that their personal reputations and livelihood might be at risk through no fault of their own. In the end, a multi-million-dollar settlement was negotiated without any significant loss of business or any unfavorable public attention. The keys to success on the communications side were identifying the real audiences, being sensitive to their emotional concerns, and striking a balance between fighting back aggressively in public, which would have only made matters worse, and trying to go into hiding, which would not have served the company's long-term strategic interest.

In most cases, keeping absolutely silent or retreating into a defensive crouch is not the best approach to take. Indeed, plaintiffs' lawyers are famous for pulling out all the stops to generate media interest and public support for their cases. They often say more in public than they would ever dare to say in the courtroom. Defense lawyers on the other hand, are often far too cautious about what they allow their clients to say before and during a trial. To be effective, litigation communications strategy must be completely coordinated with the litigation strategy itself. Communicators and lawyers must be on the same page at all times. The communications team must understand and appreciate not only the facts of the case but also the underlying legal strategy. The legal team has to be clear about how they want the communications strategy to support what they are doing on the legal side. Properly handled, litigation communication is never just a defensive exercise. Savvy lawyers appreciate this and avoid the temptation to minimize risk by saying nothing substantive outside the courtroom. They understand that "no comment" is not a realistic option in high-profile litigation. Keeping silent may at first seem like a safe approach, but it will never keep the media from covering the case or writing a story. It will just ensure that only one side of the story will be told.

Once the strategic objectives have been established and the target audiences identified, it is time to outline the case in laymen's terms. What is the case really all about, not in strictly legal terms, but from the perspective of the audiences you need to reach? Who is involved and how are they perceived by those target audiences? What are the key legal points your side wants to make? This simplified case outline is the basic tool of litigation communication. It will serve as the basis of your specific responses to anticipated questions about the case from the media and the public. It is your explanation of the case as you want the audience to understand and appreciate it. It is your key message, and you need to make sure that both the legal and communications teams are comfortable with it and that it will help you achieve your strategic communications objectives. Reducing a complicated case and a large body of evidence to a simple message outline is not easy.

For the lawyers trying the case in court every fact is important. Every angle matters. But in the court of public opinion too many facts can easily confuse the message and make it hard for ordinary people to understand. The media and the audiences you are trying to reach don't really want detailed explanations. They want simple answers to basic questions. Who did what to whom and why? The audiences you are trying to reach outside the courtroom aren't likely to pay attention to the complexities of the case, but they will respond to easily understandable messages that address their emotional concerns about the issues involved.

We once assisted a large pharmaceutical firm with communications issues involving a group of product liability cases in which the plaintiffs alleged that a drug our client sold caused cancer. The scientific and legal issues were enormously complex. Our client was prepared to argue aggressively in court that their product had nothing to do with the illness. Indeed, it was their position that their drug actually prevented other even more serious forms of cancer. But we recognized immediately that these perfectly reasonable legal positions were likely to strike the general public as an insensitive attempt to blame the innocent victims. Initial public perceptions usually favor terminally ill plaintiffs, rather than big, rich corporations.

We worked closely with the client's legal team to frame their arguments so that they would resonate with the general public. We boiled down their key message to a single word: choice. Taking our client's drug offered patients valuable therapeutic options. Cancer is bad, but options and individual choices are good. We wanted the public to focus not on the mind-numbing and highly controversial scientific details, even though we were confident that those details would win the case in court, but instead on the overall concept of options and choices, something we felt was crucial to winning the case in the court of public opinion. We wanted the public to perceive this case as being about choice, not about cancer.

We prepared every member of the legal team to translate their arguments into messages that would resonate emotionally with the general public and work the theme of choice into their answers to the questions nonlawyers were likely to ask. We did this even though it was not part of our strategy to voluntarily put lawyers forward as spokespeople outside the courtroom. We were not interested in trying the case on the courthouse steps. We just wanted to be sure that every lawyer on our side would be well prepared in case they were unable to avoid a media question. We didn't want anyone to be forced to say "no comment."

Lawyers will tell you that the most successful litigators always overprepare and under-try their cases. They are scrupulous about preparing for every possible twist and turn in the case. They insist on having answers for every possible question. They try to be ready to handle every possible issue. But when it comes time to actually stand up in the courtroom, good litigators are very careful not to overwhelm the judge and jury with every bit of material they have prepared. They understand that judges and juries are just like the rest of us. They respond best to a few important themes clearly and convincingly presented. Both inside and outside the courtroom it never pays to confuse the people who will decide your fate, or ignore what matters most to them emotionally.

9 /

Talking About Danger

The Art and Science of Risk Communication

What we now call "risk communication" is a field in which the need to reach audiences at an emotional level is particularly important. Irrational fear is always the enemy of clear thinking and effective communication. Simply explaining in rational terms why something is really not all that risky may seem like a very logical approach to the problem, but experience teaches that this rarely works in the real world. Irrational fear trumps rational thinking every time.

Communicating about risk is a difficult challenge. It means talking about danger and dealing with fear. It means explaining the unknown. It means reaching out to people who have good reason—at least, as *they* see it—to disbelieve, or even dismiss, anything you have to say. Even more than in other communications situations, effectively communicating about risk requires careful listening, something even the most sensitive communicators often find very difficult to do. But communicating effectively about risk is not impossible. There are proven principles and well-tested techniques you can use to make your point about a risky situation. First, however, it is important to examine just what we are talking about when we use the word *risk* in the first place. It is often easy to confuse the concept of *risk* with the concept of *uncertainty*. Risks can be quantified and to some extent managed. Risks can be understood and mitigated. Indeed, putting a price on risk can be very profitable, just ask any successful insurance company. Uncertainty, on the other hand, is by definition unpredictable and uncontrollable. Explaining uncontrollable uncertainty in terms of manageable risk is what successful risk communication is all about.

To an insurance underwriter, risk is the mathematical probability that something bad will happen. Risk assessment is the science of determining that probability as precisely as possible. Risk management is all about reducing unavoidable risks to safe or acceptable levels. Risk management is about harsh factual reality. Risk communication on the other hand, is all about subjective perception. Effective risk communication requires a sensitive understanding of how the people you are trying to reach perceive the risks they are forced to confront. It is a well-known, if not always well-understood, aspect of human nature that most people worry most about all the wrong things. We often ignore real risks, even as we stay up all night worrying about things that really aren't that risky at all. Most people can understand this concept intellectually, but they go on worrying anyway.

Risk Perception

Risk assessment and risk management rely on the science of numbers. Risks can be measured with statistics. Risk communication, however, has to go well beyond raw numbers. To be effective, risk communication must address opinions, attitudes, perceptions, and fears. We would all like to like to think that the facts will speak for themselves and that rational assessments based on straightforward statistical analysis will convince others to accept risk, or at least put it in proper perspective. Unfortunately, however, ordinary people rarely look at the numbers when deciding whether something is risky. They are more likely to rely on emotional perceptions when deciding how much risk they are willing to accept. That's why communicating about risk is so difficult. Because you know the facts, you may be tempted to dismiss emotional reactions to the risks associated with your organization's activities, but when it comes to someone else's willingness to accept those risks, perception is reality.

Just because our perceptions of risk are often irrational, however, doesn't mean that they can't be understood. For example, most of us perceive risks that we assume voluntarily, such as driving a car, to be far more acceptable than involuntary risks, such as breathing emissions from a nearby power plant. We choose to drive our cars, no matter how dangerous the statistical evidence shows that to be, but lots of people would avoid living next door to a power plant, even when every shred of statistical evidence clearly shows it to be perfectly safe, probably a lot safer than driving a car.

Most people perceive something to be more risky if someone else has control over it. Ask yourself whether you feel safer when you are driving the car, or when your spouse is driving and you are sitting in the passenger seat. If you have your hands on the wheel, you somehow feel safer, even if the statistical evidence clearly shows that your spouse has a far superior safe-driving record. Most of us can easily understand intellectually why we are in far greater danger driving to the airport than flying in an airplane. The statistical evidence is clear and unequivocal, but we still tend to feel a lot more concerned about our safety in the air than on the road. It may be irrational, but most of us worry a lot more about situations where we are not in control. And risks that are associated with clear benefits, such as the mobility afforded by driving a car, usually worry us much less than those where there is no obvious personal benefit, such as living next door to that power plant.

We once represented the manufacturer of a synthetic growth hormone that is very popular with dairy farmers who give it to their cows to make them give more milk. This is not the sort of thing you would expect to generate a huge public outcry. But it did, and the reason was really very simple. As the manufacturer constantly tried to argue, their synthetic growth hormone has absolutely no effect on the milk itself. It just makes the cows give more of it, thereby increasing the farmer's profits. And that, of course, was the key to the puzzle. Farmers get all the benefit from giving their cows synthetic growth hormones. Consumers get none at all. The consumer activists who mounted a campaign against the growth hormone never were called upon to prove that the hormone was actually dangerous. They simply had to ask consumers whether they were willing to accept any risk at all, given that they were not sharing any benefit. Nobody thinks twice about adding vitamin D to milk or iodine to salt. Indeed, unlike the growth hormone given to dairy cows, both vitamin D and iodine are additives that consumers actually ingest. But both are also clearly understood to be beneficial. In the absence of strong evidence to the contrary, our natural instinct is to focus on the benefit and ignore the risk. It is all about emotional perception, rather than scientific fact.

Moreover, facts and statistics notwithstanding, most people

tend to be more concerned about new and unfamiliar risks than they are about those that have been around for awhile. For example, the facts clearly show that a nuclear power plant is far les risky to its neighbors than an old fashioned coal-fired plant. Yet, how many people do you know who would feel as comfortable with the new and unfamiliar risk of odorless, tasteless, and colorless radiation supposedly coming from a nuclear plant than they are with the old, familiar black smoke that pours out of a coal plant?

Or, consider the worldwide controversy that has raged over genetically modified food products. The technical term is agricultural biotechnology, not to be confused with biotechnology as it is applied to the development and manufacture of new pharmaceuticals. Activist opponents of agricultural biotechnology, however, prefer the term *Frankenfood,* suggesting, of course, that food grown from genetically modified seeds is somehow monstrous and risky. We first got involved in the agricultural biotechnology controversy as it was emerging in the United States after sweeping Europe.

As is so often the case in difficult risk communications situations, supporters of agricultural biotechnology had the scientific facts firmly on their side. There has never been any credible scientific evidence that food grown from genetically modified seeds is any different than food grown from familiar, unmodified seeds. But that was part of the problem. Proponents of genetic modification of crops, like those who earlier supported growth hormones for dairy cows, can't point to any direct benefit of the technology for consumers. Genetically engineered plants that are modified to resist pests and allow for less frequent applications of chemical pesticides are very good for farmers, but the food crops that are eventually harvested are indistinguishable from those grown from conventional seeds. They aren't any more dangerous, but neither are they any less expensive, or any more nutritious. There is no direct benefit to consumers, and no credible answer to the ultimate question, "what if?"

So it should come as no surprise that the increasingly noisy chorus of antibiotech activists kept asking consumers why they should have to take any risk at all if the new technology offered them no personal benefit. This is called the "precautionary principle." And for those trying to communicate rationally about risk, the precautionary principle—the "what if?" question—is a dangerous trap. It's a question that nobody who lacks the gift of prophecy can possibly answer. But that doesn't mean it won't play well at public demonstrations and in the media.

Companies trying to market genetically modified seeds in Europe were also victims of very bad timing. It wasn't their fault that European regulators had just been thoroughly discredited by their clumsy handling of the sudden and very frightening outbreak of "mad cow disease." Especially in Britain, government regulators made every possible communications mistake. First they ignored the problem. Then, when disturbing pictures of stumbling cows and horrible stories about the suffering of human victims began to proliferate in the media, regulators chose to offer unwise and unsupportable assurances that the situation was well under control. Remember the staged publicity pictures of a smiling British minister feeding his young daughter a hamburger? Finally, when all the overconfident official assurances began to be swamped by more and more stories of mad cow disease outbreaks, human victims, and bureaucratic ineptitude, the public's trust in government regulation of food safety evaporated. Hardly the best time to be introducing a new food technology that depended on government approval to be accepted by the public.

Most unfortunate, however, was the way that the agricultural biotech companies went about addressing all these difficult issues as they began introducing their new technology to the European market. Their messages were as blunt as they were ineffective. We're scientists. We're smarter than you are. Trust us. You have nothing to worry about, and don't trust anyone who says you do. This is exactly what anyone trying to deal with fear of the unknown should never do. The results were swift, predictable, and devastating. Even though European farmers understood perfectly well that there was nothing at all dangerous about genetically modified seeds, they didn't dare use it for fear their crops would be rejected in the marketplace. Before long, the issue was settled by the European Union which put in place regulations banning the sale of anything grown from genetically modified seeds. It took years for those regulations to be relaxed, and even now a residue of deep public distrust remains. This was a classic example of failed risk communication.

Luckily, our clients in the United States were still in a position to avoid the disaster that befell their counterparts in Europe. At the time we got involved in the issue, the *Frankenfood* story had still not captured the media's imagination nearly as much as it had overseas, and the American public's trust in government regulation of the food supply was still high. But that nagging "what if?" question still remained, and the antibiotech activists were not a bit shy about asking it. Studies that the activists claimed had shown that endangered monarch butterflies were being poisoned by pollen from genetically modified corn plants were quickly debunked, but little children dressed up as monarch butterflies were already starting to show up at our client's plants, ready to fall over on cue and pretend to die for the cameras. The media were starting to show an all too predictable, if largely uninformed, interest in the story.

Using public opinion research and focus groups, we were able to determine that American opinion about the safety of genetically modified crops was still fluid. A small percentage of the public was unalterably opposed to agricultural biotechnology and outraged that so much genetically engineered food was already on the shelves. But most of the public and the media had never even heard of the technology. They were unaware, and therefore unconcerned, that an enormous percentage of many important crops like soybeans was already being grown from genetically modified seeds, without any discernable negative impact on human health or safety.

Those who had heard about the technology but were still undecided about it were, for the most part, very poorly informed. In one focus group, for example, a woman who was not particularly concerned about the safety of genetically modified crops in general had heard stories about experiments in which genes from an arctic fish were supposedly inserted into tomato plants in order to keep the fruit from freezing. That story was untrue, but it caused this woman to be concerned that her tomatoes would start smelling like fish, something she found very unpleasant. That level of public ignorance usually presents both a challenge and an opportunity. On the one hand, people who know little about a new and complex technology, but are not yet afraid of it, are usually open to education. That certainly seemed to be the case in this situation. At the same time, however, the other side has just as good a chance of making the audience believe that the technology is dangerous as you have of convincing them that it is safe. Initial perceptions are hard to reverse, and time is of the essence.

Taking advantage of the trustworthy reputation of American food regulators, who had long since approved agricultural biotechnology for use and sale in this country, and arranging key explanatory interviews with mass-media outlets, we were able to neutralize much of the negative publicity that the other side was trying so hard to generate. We did not attempt to debate opponents of agricultural biotechnology on their own emotional turf. That would only have served to make us look defensive. Nor did we try to discredit the other side's televised publicity stunts. That would have made it look like we didn't care about the serious safety concerns they were raising. We tried instead to educate the broader public about the new technology, while remaining sensitive to their values and their concerns about food safety.

The situation we faced with agricultural biotechnology was not all that unusual. When assessing risk and deciding what to worry about, most people consider perceptual factors such as benefit, control, and familiarity to be far more important than scientific facts, no matter how persuasive those facts may be to those who understand and appreciate their meaning and significance. Scientists and engineers may not like it, but scientific facts mean little or nothing to those who believe they are being forced to breathe dirty air or eat strange food.

In this connection, it is interesting to note that the controversy that to some extent still surrounds genetic modification in agriculture never grew up around exactly the same technology when it was used to create new drugs. An overwhelming majority of the public, in the United States and abroad, has always considered pharmaceutical biotechnology to be a miracle, even if they consider the very same technology when applied to agriculture as a threat to life as we know it on the planet. Again, it is all about who takes the risk and who benefits from it. Most of us consider pharmaceuticals, however they are manufactured, to be essentially beneficial. New drugs that promise to cure deadly diseases benefit all mankind. But, so far at least, genetically modified crops directly benefit only the farmers that grow them. In coming years, when genetic modification produces crops that deliver understandable benefits, such as better nutrition and reduced fat, that matter to the rest of us, whatever controversy still remains about genetically modified food is likely to fade away.

Who Is in Control?

When laying out a risk communications strategy it is also important to understand that many arguments about risk are really not about risk at all. They are about power and control. They are about who decides whether a particular risk is acceptable or unacceptable, and whether something is useful enough to be worth taking any risk at all. Therefore, making people feel they are being listened to respectfully, that they are valued participants in the decision-making process, is an essential element of effective risk communication. Effective risk communication is often a matter of giving power to the powerless, involving those likely to be most affected, and therefore most worried, so that they don't feel forgotten in an unfamiliar and uncomfortable situation. As those American biotechnology companies that tried to muscle genetically modified seeds onto the European market learned the hard way, no risk message you present, however well supported by the available scientific facts, will ever be successful if it makes you appear to be forcing others to accept your point of view. Your mission is to inform. It is better to leave the decision making, or even the perception of decision making, to your audience. They will decide soon enough whether to accept or reject what you say about the risks you are asking them to accept. And they will make that crucial decision largely on the basis of their own values, fears, doubts, and perceptions, rather than on the basis of any scientific facts you give them, however solid those facts might be.

Breaking through the barrier of emotion and perception isn't easy. The most important step in communicating about risk is building and maintaining bridges to the public, bridges that demand constant maintenance. If this relationship of trust has been established and maintained, honest risk communication at least has a chance of being accepted by the public. Without trust and credibility, however, there is little chance that any message, no matter how scientifically accurate, will be believed or accepted. Effective risk communication must address perceptions. It must reach the heart and the gut before it can possibly reach the head. However uncomfortable it may be, and however irrational it may sometimes seem, you must first respect and appreciate your audience's emotional perceptions if you are to have any chance of changing their minds.

Let's go back to those people living next door to the nuclear power plant. Why in the world are they so worried? Don't they know that nobody in this country has ever died as the result of a nuclear power plant accident? Are people who live near nuclear plants somehow just dumber than the rest of us? Has all that mysterious radiation somehow scrambled their brains? Of course not. It is simply human nature. These people are reacting the way any of us would in the same situation, no matter how capable we might be of understanding the risks we face at a technical level. They are reacting emotionally, even irrationally, because that's what human beings do, especially when they fear that their lives or those of their families might be at risk.

What We Know and What We Feel

Before dismissing all this as just another example of public ignorance fed by media sensationalism, remember that polls have shown more Americans believe in the virgin birth than believe in evolution. It is difficult to imagine that all these good people are so completely ignorant of modern science. But it shouldn't be all that hard to accept that, while they may understand evolution, not to mention modern scientific breakthroughs like embryonic stem cell research and cloning, Americans still take their religious beliefs seriously, so seriously that they are willing to set aside intellectual understanding in favor of something more emotionally conforting and spiritually satisfying.

Over the years, the art and science of risk communication has gone through several stages of evolution. At first it was thought that all the problems associated with communicating about risk were simply a matter of explanation: If technical people would just explain risks clearly, the theory went, intelligent people would understand and stop worrying. That theory certainly seemed to make sense on the surface, but it failed miserably in actual practice. Attempting to deal with irrational fears by explaining potentially dangerous situations in rational terms may seem like a sensible approach to a scientist, but it completely ignores human nature. Just try explaining to someone with a pathological fear of heights why standing next to the window in a skyscraper isn't really dangerous. Those of us who are afraid of heights know perfectly well that we are very unlikely to fall out of a closed window, but that doesn't make us any less fearful. Our phobia about heights is not grounded in any actual danger. It is, by definition, irrational. Trying to explain away irrational fear in rational terms is a waste of time.

When rational explanation failed, risk communicators turned to translation. The notion was that ordinary people were tuning out factual messages about risk because the experts insisted on using big words and fancy technical arguments in an effort to put risk in its proper scientific perspective. This also seemed like a sensible approach, but it, too, stubbornly ignored the enormous importance of irrational human nature. It doesn't matter how elegantly you translate a highly technical explanation into laymen's terms, it is still a rational explanation going up against an irrational fear, and irrational fear is bound to win every time.

Today, risk communication has become a lot more sophisticated and a lot more in tune with human nature. It is still important to translate all the jargon and communicate in familiar terms. But it is far more important to address the issue of control by involving the people who feel themselves to be at risk in the process of putting that risk into its proper perspective. The process is sometimes called "mutual gains," and it is a classic win-win bargaining approach that has been used quite successfully in a variety of situations, including labor disputes, environmental negotiations, and other debates about relative risk.

The process is simple and powerful:

- First you must acknowledge and respect the values and concerns of the people you are trying to reach. Take time to listen to what worries them. Try to understand the situation on their terms. Don't be like those arrogant corporations that tried to force genetically modified crops into the skeptical European market. Don't act like you have all the answers and the other side is simply too stupid to understand them. You may be right on the facts, but the people you are trying to reach will always have the last word. Facts are only helpful if the people you are trying to reach are willing to listen, and if those scientific facts ring true to the audience.

- Involve the people with whom you are trying to communicate in the fact-finding process. It is part of our shared human nature that we are far more likely to believe something we have discovered for ourselves than something we are forced to accept from someone else. If Europeans had been given an opportunity to gain their own understanding of genetically modified seeds without the pressure of an arrogant American salesman telling them they didn't know what was good for them, they might have had fewer concerns about the technology when it was first introduced, and American biotech companies trying to get into the European market would not still be playing catch-up.

- Make a credible commitment to minimize the impact of anything that might eventually go wrong. It is simply not credible to claim that absolutely nothing bad is ever going to happen. Even the best laid plans sometimes go awry. Even the most miraculous technology sometimes delivers unpleasant surprises. Acknowledging the possibility, however remote, that something could go wrong, will help bolster your credibility. Working with other interested parties to develop plans for dealing with worst-case scenarios gets everyone who has a stake in the outcome involved right from the start. Nobody comes out of the process feeling that their concerns were ignored or their values disrespected.

- Accept responsibility for whatever risks there may be. For example, if your company owns a nuclear plant, and the neighbors are worried that it might be a risk to their health and safety, don't try to divert responsibility for the plant's safety operation to state or federal regulators. It is often very tempting to tell anyone who will listen that your plant "meets all applicable regulatory guidelines." But to your worried neighbors that just sounds like you are hiding behind the letter of the law. It certainly won't make them feel any safer. The Three Mile Island plant was in total compliance with all the regulations, too, until something went terribly wrong.

Giving Up Control

Remember that risk perception is more about power and control than about actual danger. People who feel they have no control over a situation just naturally feel it is more threatening, even when the facts suggest the opposite. So be prepared to share power. Make sure that risk communication is always a two-way process. And always play the long game. Work at building long-term relationships with those who have a stake.

Mark Twain was right when he said that when you need a friend it is too late to make one. For example, several years ago we worked on crisis planning with one of our clients who operated a relatively small meatpacking plant. Unlike most such operations, which are usually located in industrial areas, this plant happened to be right in the middle of a quiet urban neighborhood. In fact, it was just across the street from an elementary school. Like most meatpacking plants, this one had large coolers that used ammonia gas as a refrigerant. Ammonia is great for refrigeration, but if the gas leaks it can be highly flammable and very poisonous. Ammonia leaks and fires are a well-understood risk that all meatpacking plants face. This plant was operating safely and was well prepared to deal with anything that might unexpectedly go wrong.

But as prepared as they were to deal with emergencies on their own property, the plant managers had never given any thought to the school across the street. They knew it was there, of course, and they certainly understood the danger that an ammonia leak, fire, or explosion would pose for the children and their teachers. But they had never thought to discuss those dangers with the school. Since nothing had ever gone wrong, the plant managers weren't even sure that the school was aware of the potential danger just across the street. The people who ran the school and the people who ran the plant might never have met one another, until they found themselves in the middle of a life-and-death emergency. That is not the best time to start making friends or building long-term relationships.

We advised our client to reach out to the school and invite teachers and administrators to visit the plant and see for themselves what went on inside so they could evaluate the risk for themselves. Above all, we urged the plant managers to get the school directly involved in the ongoing emergency and crisis planning process. Being completely open about the actual risks always helps make those risks seem less mysterious and therefore of less concern. Bringing the neighbors into the process of planning for an emergency response gives them something useful to do in the event of an actual incident. Better to have those who have the most cause to be concerned ready to help you handle the problem, rather than keep them outside the process with nothing to do but criticize your response.

Putting It All Together

To illustrate how the risk communication process works in practice, imagine that you are the manager of a large chemical plant,

and consider how you would work through the following hypothetical example of one of the most difficult challenges in the risk
communication field—telling your story to a neighboring community concerned about the health and safety risks posed by your
operation.

First you need to know what you are talking about. Make sure
you have all the relevant data about your plant, its operations, and
emissions close at hand. Make sure the information is up-to-date.
Work with your safety, medical, health, and environmental management teams to analyze and assess all the relevant information
about the plant's emissions and other hazards.

When you are satisfied that you have the facts, personalize and
simplify your message. Remember to frame the information not
just in a way that makes sense to you, but in terms that will resonate with your target audience. For example, describing a particular risk using terms such as "ten to the minus sixteen" may seem
obvious to you, but it is probably way too technical for the audience you need to reach. Rather than addressing the concerns of a
skeptical audience, this kind of technical information, on its own,
is more likely to send the unintended message that you are hiding
something truly dangerous behind an opaque curtain of technical
jargon. There are many ways of talking about health and safety
data without getting too technical, and the simplest approach is
almost always the best.

Be careful with illustrative risk comparisons. Comparisons
that make sense to you might generate a surprisingly negative reaction on the part of the audience. This often happens when you
try to describe something undeniably risky in terms of something
perfectly safe and ordinary. If, for example, you try to compare
the fine particles of soot that a diesel engine puts into the air to
the crumbs that fall off a burnt piece of toast, you wouldn't be

very far off technically, but the analogy probably wouldn't have the intended calming effect on your audience. Toast is tasty. Diesel smoke is scary. Using one to describe the other is likely to strike an already fearful audience as either just a bit too clever or, worse, somewhat arrogant and cavalier.

Explain in simple terms the steps you have taken to reduce the chance of emergencies and deal with any spills or leaks that may occur. Again, one of the primary goals of all risk communication is to minimize irrational fear and put any real risks in their proper perspective. Describe your emergency prevention and response planning in terms that matter to the community. Describe what you are doing to reduce emissions, what recent measurements show, and where people can get additional information.

Even though the media may sometimes try to stir up fear because it makes for a better story, the people who live around your chemical plant—the people you are trying to reach with your message—just want to feel safe and secure. They may come to the process with doubts and concerns, but they are probably more than willing to listen to a credible and sincere message about what is being done to keep them safe. When you go to the doctor for your annual checkup, are you disappointed if he finds nothing wrong but still sends you a bill? Of course not. What you really want, and what you are more than willing to pay for, is a clean bill of health.

Review your industrial hygiene and emergency response programs and be prepared to explain the measures you are taking to protect both workers and the community from accidents. Prepare in advance simplified information sheets that communicate clearly with the media and the public, in familiar terms and plain language, about your products and hazardous materials. Explain the OSHA and EPA standards that apply to your plant. Obtain monitoring and modeling information to show that facility and neighborhood exposures are lower than government standards. But don't stop there. Explain how you have kept exposures low and how you will continue to do so.

Discuss health effects data as they affect employees and the community. Use concrete language. For example, you may explain that the data show that when a certain number of laboratory animals are exposed to a specific amount of a particular chemical in a certain way, they exhibit a certain response or no response at all. Explain that you are controlling exposure to workers at a level a hundred times lower than that, and to the public at a level a thousand times lower. Use charts, graphs, slides, and videotapes to make your key points. Thanks largely to the work of graphic arts experts who prepare visual aids for use in the courtroom, there are now an enormous number of powerful tools available to make even the most complex scientific and technical information understandable to ordinary people. Pictures and animation can indeed be worth many thousands of words.

Risk communication, like emergency response, is a team effort. Make sure to include experts from your safety and health, legal, environmental, communications, and personnel departments in the process right from the start. Turn to industrial hygienists, toxicologists, and physicians to quantify your plant's emissions and help you develop credible health messages. No matter how much technical expertise you bring to bear on the problem, however, you must always make the information relevant to your audience. As with any communications exercise, you need to know who you are trying to persuade and what concerns they have, before you can communicate with them effectively. And it is always best to respond to the audience's feelings before addressing substantive matters. Acknowledging that "I can tell you're angry about this" won't make the anger go away, but it will enable you to focus more clearly on the substantive issues at hand, and it will send a powerful message that you are sincerely trying to communicate, not just lecture a scientifically ignorant audience.

Start by working with your own employees. Don't assume that employees and their families will automatically understand or believe what you say. And you certainly can't order anyone to just shut up and not be afraid. If you have failed to establish credibility with your own employees, they may well turn out to be negative ambassadors to the rest of the community, giving outsiders good reason to be even more fearful than they otherwise would have been. If, on the other hand, you involve your employees in the risk communication process, they will become your best spokespeople. When they go back out into the community every night you want them to be talking about safety and benefits, not danger and risk.

Community surveys, employee questionnaires, and media background interviews can help you determine how people in the community really feel about your plant and help you identify the concerns you need to address. When reaching out to the community it is best to talk with small groups. Avoid large, open community meetings where you may become a target for emotional attacks by disgruntled employees or activist groups. It is rarely possible to communicate effectively with an angry mob. Involve community leaders in your planning. A local emergency planning committee is an ideal group with which to begin communicating about any risks associated with your facility. This audience has a stake in knowing what goes on at the plant, as well as how and why.

Be conservative. Avoid the temptation to promise too much or paint an unrealistically rosy picture of the hazards associated with your plant. For example, don't promise zero emissions if you can't possibly deliver. Never be afraid to acknowledge uncertainty.

Explain that detection always outruns correction. Discuss problems with modeling, measuring, and interpreting data in simple terms. Don't be afraid to admit that there are things you don't know.

Work with the media. The media are not your primary audience, but they are often the key to communicating risk to the community. The media may seem uninformed, argumentative, and annoying at times, but cooperating with them will yield a more accurate and balanced interpretation of your data than will an adversarial relationship. Get help. Communicating about risk is hard work and should never be attempted alone. It requires personnel, time, and money. Consider enlisting the assistance of local authorities, professors, health officials, and emergency planning professionals. They can help you figure out how best to communicate complex issues to the public and may even be willing to participate in your presentations to community groups. Take a step-by-step approach. Nothing as complicated as risk communication can be handled overnight. Start by making a list of the necessary activities for a risk communications program and begin delegating responsibility for specific projects. Your initial list could include hazardous material information sheets, community surveys, employee questionnaires, risk comparisons, risk communications visuals, basic plant data, community group meetings, local emergency planning committee meetings, and media backgrounders.

Finally, remember that there are real risks beyond the familiar explosions, fires, leaks, and spills for which most companies spend most of their time and energy preparing. In the age of the Internet, risks such as identity theft and loss of critical data are very real and cause ordinary people great concern. So try running through this hypothetical risk communication example again, but this time imagine yourself as the operator of a Web site rather than a chemical plant. What do visitors to your site worry about?

How can you assure them that the personal information they give you will be secure? How can you make them understand that giving a credit card number to a Web site is really no more dangerous than handing the card itself to a waiter in a restaurant? How can you communicate effectively the balance between the risks and benefits inherent in e-commerce? The fundamental communications challenges are the same as those associated with the chemical plant. No matter how far technology may advance, people are still going to worry about all the wrong things. Risk communication is all about reassuring other people that the worst is unlikely to happen and that you are well prepared to handle the situation if it does.

A Final Word

I t may come as a surprise to those who take today's high-speed communications networks for granted as a daily companion for work and entertainment, but the first digital communications device was the ordinary telegraph, put into commercial service well before the Civil War. The dots and dashes of the Morse code that telegraph operators used for more than a century are essentially the same as the binary digits that modern computers understand. The only difference between a telegraph wire and a fiber optic cable is what we now call bandwidth, the number of dots and dashes, or digital 1s and 0s that can travel together simultaneously. Back when Samuel F. B. Morse sent his famous telegraph message, "What hath God wrought," he was dealing with a bandwidth of only a single digit. While a dash was moving down the wire, the dot had to wait its turn. Today's big bandwidth digital pipes aren't all that different from yesterday's copper telegraph wires, except that they can carry billions of 1s and 0s side by side.

Communications technology may have come a long way in a short time, but the basic principles haven't changed all that much since early humans first began gesturing and grunting at one another during a hunt. After all this time, human communication should be no mystery. It remains one of the most basic of our day-to-day activities. We all communicate with each other constantly in one-on-one encounters with family and friends, meetings with business associates, PowerPoint presentations to small groups, and sometimes even speeches to audiences of hundreds or thousands. From routine telephone calls with reporters to on-camera interviews and perhaps even more challenging crisis communication situations, many of us have had an opportunity at some point in our careers to deal with the media.

It should be clear by now that whatever the circumstances, and no matter how high the stakes, successful communication depends on a carefully developed strategy as well as practical tools and tactics. Moreover, even in the most difficult and dangerous situations, communication should always be seen as an opportunity as well as a challenge. As we have seen throughout this book, successful communication is always positive and proactive. There are a host of purely defensive techniques you can use to deflect tough questions and spin negative stories. Indeed, the most obvious defense is not to communicate at all. But silence is rarely an option in the real world. And none of these defensive tactics will do much to help you get people to pay attention, believe what you say, or remember the point you want to make. The truth well told is always more effective than even the most clever spin. Defensive tactics won't change the way people think or feel. They won't help you change anyone's mind.

Regardless of the situation and no matter what the medium, effective communication is always a two-way proposition. As we've learned from Aristotle, effective communication is as much about listening as talking, and it is always more about what matters to your audience than what matters to you. It is always more about what your audience hears and perceives than it is about what you actually say. Above all, effective communication depends on a sensitive understanding and appreciation of what motivates an audience emotionally, not so much what they know as what they feel and believe. Communication is a very human activity and at the end of the day it is all about human nature.

By now you know the basic steps. Look carefully at the situation. What are the challenges and opportunities you face? What is your objective. What do you hope to accomplish? Think through your strategy. Know why you want to communicate, as well as what you want to say. Understand your audience. Be sensitive to their attitudes, emotions, and expectations. And above all, know the point you want to make and be prepared to use every tactical tool at your disposal to make it.